GW00683475

To Be Chasidic

To Be Chasidic

A CONTEMPORARY GUIDE

CHAIM DALFIN

JASON ARONSON INC.
Northvale, New Jersey
London

This book was set in 12 pt. Garamond by AeroType, Inc.

10   9   8   7   6   5   4   3   2   1

Library of Congress Cataloging-in-Publication Data

Dalfin, Chaim.
    To be chasidic : a contemporary guide / Chaim Dalfin.
      p. cm.
    Includes bibliographical references and index.
    ISBN 1-56821-905-9 (alk. paper)
    1. Hasidism.   2. Jewish way of life. I. Title.
BM198.2.D35   1996
296.8'332—dc20

                                       96-13673
                                         CIP

Manufactured in the United States of America. Jason Aronson Inc. offers books and cassettes. For information and a catalog write to Jason Aronson Inc., 230 Livingston Street, Northvale, New Jersey 07647.

To my dear parents
Reb Aron Hillel and Miriam Dalfin

who gave me freedom while raising me
with the ideals of Chasidism
who gave encouragement and inspiration
to my writing
who continue to support the goals of Chasidus.

May you see only *Yiddishe* and *Chasidshe nachas*
from your children and grandchildren,
and may you proclaim with a sense of pride and joy,
"See the children that I have raised"
(Tractate *Kesubos* 45a).

Contents

Acknowledgments

When one wants to thank people for their assistance, one realizes how insufficient the thanks are. Whatever one can say will only express a glimpse of the true and deep feelings of the heart. To all those who gave of themselves to help spread the ideals of Torah and *mitzvos,* the true thanks will come from God Almighty, who is limitless and infinite. It is God who truly "pays back" and whose blessing truly means something.

To begin with, I say thanks to God, who gave me the strength to persevere in this work. It is God who gives strength. All He asks is that we allow His blessing to enter. Fortunate are those who make themselves a *keli,* a vessel, to receive and to acknowledge that it all comes from Him.

I wish for each and every one who assisted in the book becoming a reality, that God's *brocha,* which is infinite, be bestowed upon you and your families. I do want to mention several people in particular for special recognition.

First is our dear and beloved Rebbe Menachem Mendel Schneerson of blessed memory, whose teachings and directives are alive now, more than before. The Rebbe did not just leave us a legacy; he lives on through the study and practice of his teachings, which I attempt to share with you in the book. As a student and *chasid,* I was honored to experience firsthand how one leads a chasidic life-style, from the master *chasid* par excellence, the Rebbe, who was and is our leader.

Within the chasidic movement there are the teachings of Chasidus, and the practices and customs of Chasidus. The latter are the ultimate expression of living as a *chasid;* however, it is necessary to have an understanding of what Chasidus is all about. The individual who spent hours sharing, teaching and explaining Chasidus to my contemporaries and myself is Reb Yoel Kahan, the Lubavitcher Rebbe's *chozer* (the repeater, who memorizes the Rebbe's words and reviews them with the *chasidim*). Reb Yoel contributed to this book by answering questions and by giving suggestions on the presentation of various topics. Thank you, Reb Yoel, for all of your help.

Special thanks go to my parents, Reb Aron Hillel and Miriam Dalfin, who gave me my foundation and continue to strengthen it; my dear wife, Bashi, who read the manuscript and made critical comments, greatly improving the book; my five children, Menachem Mendel, Shterna Sara, Brocha, Hinda Fraida, and Chaya Mushka, who constantly kept me on my feet, making the combination of writing and family responsibilities a real test, which all of us have benefitted from; my brother Anshel and Yossi Greenbaum, who continue to support my endeavors; my paternal grandparents of blessed memory, Reb Shlomo and Baila Dalfin, and my maternal grandparents of blessed memory, Reb Shlomo Menashe and Hinda Fraida Wiroslow, who were *chasidim* and would always tell me chasidic stories of their rebbes in Poland and Romania, adding inspiration to follow the chasidic life-style. May this book contribute to the eternal bliss that they experience in the world of truth.

I want to express my appreciation to Mr. Arthur Kurzweil and the rest of the staff at Jason Aronson Inc., who realized the potential of the manuscript and made it a reality; Professor Herman Branover and Rabbi Abraham Twerski for reviewing and endorsing the book; my good friend Rabbi Yanky Winner, *Mashpia* of the *Yeshivah Gedolah* in Melbourne, Australia, who spent many hours adding significant points to many chapters; Mr. Avrohom Modes, who edited the manuscript using his vast background of Jewish and secular studies; Rabbi Issar Zalman Weissberg, Dr. Judy Mishell, Mrs. Devorah Kreiman, Mr. Gavriel Fleiderman, and Mr. Shlomo Dersh, who took time from their busy schedules to read the manuscript and give valuable feedback. Finally, I thank all those whose names escape me. May each and every one of you be blessed.

May this book be received and viewed as a stepping-stone toward the fulfillment of *Moshiach*'s response to the Baal Shem Tov: "When are you coming? When your wellsprings will be spread to the outside world!" Amen, may it be now!

Introduction

MOSHE RABBEINU, MOSHE'S TORAH

Traditional Judaism has been around for over three thousand years. Moshe, our teacher and leader, communicated to the children of Israel not only the written Torah but also the Oral Law. In fact, our Rabbis teach us in the Jerusalem Talmud (Tractate *Pe'ah,* Chapter 2, *Halachah* 4) that whatever novelty a person discovers in studying Torah, Moshe Rabbeinu had received that insight on Mount Sinai. This is hard to understand. Since the student studies diligently and uses his mind to understand the depth of Torah, why shouldn't he be credited with the new insight! Yet the tradition gives the credit to Moshe.

The reason for this is that Moshe was the servant of God and therefore the Torah is called *Toras Moshe* (Malachi 3:22). Torah was made accessible only through Moshe, who had self-sacrifice for Torah. It was Moshe who put his life on the line by accepting the task of leading the Jewish people out of Egypt and who received the Torah despite the difficulties he knew were ahead. Even at the Red Sea, some groups suggested suicide, while others considered going back to Egypt! Moshe continued going forward. While traveling in the desert, they complained about not having meat, but Moshe persevered.

Because of all this, Moshe knew quite well who he was dealing with, yet he dedicated his life for the children of Israel. He was chosen to be the person who had a "private audience" with God for forty days and nights. Moshe paid his dues, not only spiritually, but practically, by not eating and sleeping for forty days and nights. He sat as a student, learning the Torah in its entirety, the exoteric and esoteric, including the general rules of Torah, the axioms that are the foundation for insights and novelties for all of eternity. This is why Moshe is credited with the Torah being called "His Torah," *Toras Moshe.*

WHAT BROUGHT ABOUT THE TEACHINGS OF CHASIDUS?

There are two major reasons for the recent introduction of Chasidus in the early 1700s. The first has to do with the troubles of the era immediately preceding.

Jewish people for centuries have been living their lives in accordance with Torah and its Oral Laws. Generally speaking, Jewish people never questioned the validity of Torah and the words of the Rabbis. In fact, the Torah's instruction, "you shall not deviate to the right or the left," is explained by Rashi to be a specific command to follow the words of the Rabbis as interpreted in the Oral Torah. However, with the impact of physical and spiritual oppression in the 1600s, such as the Chelminitzky pogroms and false messiahs, Jewish people began doubting the authenticity of Torah. They felt they were the target of God's wrath, a human scapegoat singled out for destruction. This caused them to give up and forsake the Torah. They couldn't continue relying on the legalistic interpretations within the Talmud. They felt the Rabbis had let them down and the Torah was outdated. As time progressed, observance of Torah declined, and not just among the ignorant. There was a need for a spiritual awakening, to bring Jews back to God and his Torah.

Along came Rabbi Yisroel Baal Shem Tov, who revealed the inner beauty of Torah, which he called Chasidus. The Baal Shem taught that God wasn't limited to those that were knowledgeable in Talmud or came from distinguished backgrounds. Rather, what makes a Jew is the Jewish *neshomah*—soul. Regardless of one's achievement in Torah or lack thereof, a Jew is a Jew. In fact, the talmudic scholar is not necessarily closer to God than the ignoramus. As a matter of fact, the opposite is quite possible, because the scholar has the pride associated with knowledge, while the simpleton may be humble and sincere.

The Baal Shem's novel approach revolutionized all of Jewry. His teachings came as a surprise to the establishment. They were walking around thinking of themselves as God's gift to humanity, and then they found out that they were no better than the next Jew. Their Torah study, if it had been an expression of their ego and pride, was repulsive in God's eyes! As the Talmud clearly states, ''I [God] can't dwell in the same room as him [the arrogant person]!'' (*Eirchin* 15b). This creative insight was initially frowned upon by many. On further investigation into the doctrines and behavior of the Baal Shem and his disciples, his ideas received eminence and were recognized by many former opponents to be the inner meaning of normative Torah Judaism. These scholars discovered a new emotional and spiritual dimension that gave life to their formerly cold and dry studies.

The second reason has to do with the fact that as time goes on, the Messianic Era gets closer. What does this have to do with the revelation of Chasidus? The law is that on *Erev Shabbos* (Friday), one should taste the food that has been prepared for *Shabbos.* Since the days of Moshiach are called ''*Yom Shekulo Shabbos*'' (end of tractate *Tamid,* 33b, Rashi on *Tehillim* 92:1), a day that is completely *Shabbos,* therefore in the time prior to the messianic millennium, that is, the second half of the sixth millennium, we ''taste'' the food of *Shabbos,* that food being *Pnimiyus haTorah,* the inner esoteric teachings of Torah. The reason *Pnimiyus haTorah* is considered the food of *Shabbos* is that during Moshiach's time, we will be studying the secrets of Torah, as stated by the Rambam (Laws of Kings and Their Wars 12:5). Just as ''water covers the sea,'' so, too, will the knowledge of God fill the world. Therefore, the Baal Shem Tov began sharing his teachings in the era immediately prior to *Shabbos.*

THE AUTHOR'S BACKGROUND

It is the philosophical and practical chasidic teachings that have inspired me to write this book. When one is dedicated to a certain Torah life-style and believes that everyone can benefit from it, one has an obligation to share it. That is why I wrote this book. It is my personal conviction and love for Chasidus that drove me to put feelings into writing so that others can benefit from it. I was raised as a *chasid.* My parents are *chasidim,* and both my paternal and maternal grandparents and their grandparents were *chasidim.* I studied in chasidic *yeshivos* and made it my business to have discussions about all issues of life, from the spiritual to the physical, with *chasidim.*

Together with my strong sense of living a chasidic life-style, I am fully aware of the thousands of Jews who are not chasidic and are truly God-fearing, adhering to the details of Torah. If so, why is it necessary to study and practice Chasidus? To answer the question I need to first explain basic philosophies of Judaism and then show the richness of the contributions that Chasidus has given Traditional Judaism. This approach will also explore the quality that Chasidus gives to those who are already learning Torah and practicing the details of Judaism.

This is why the title of the book is *To Be Chasidic: A Contemporary Guide.* It is my goal to demonstrate how one can incorporate chasidic practices and customs into contemporary life.

TRADITIONAL JUDAISM, NOT ORTHODOX JUDAISM

Throughout the book I have chosen the phrase "Traditional Jew," instead of "Orthodox Jew," to describe the normative attitude towards Torah and *mitzvos* of all observant Jews. In today's Jewish world, it is important to let people know that there is one Judaism. Some do more, some do less; however, all are Jews. There is but one tradition—Judaism. Some add one nuance and others add another nuance, but the kernel is the same. Chasidism is one way of expressing the very essence of traditional Judaism.

One Tradition

It is also important to mention that, as a general rule, I have chosen not to make distinctions within Traditional Judaism itself, even though I am aware of the multiple facets of the so-called Orthodox movement. There is Modern Orthodox, Centrist Orthodox, Right and Left Wing Orthodox; there is the nonchasidic community, also known as the misnagdic community; there is the Torah U'Mada community; there are the Sefardim; and the list goes on and on. The same is true in the chasidic community—there are literally hundreds of different chasidic groups.

Because of all these different approaches, I've generally chosen to keep it simple and not get into the differences. Traditional Judaism is an umbrella term to cover those who follow the *halachah* as set forth in the Code of Jewish Law, without venturing into the teachings and practices of Chasidism and Kabbalah. Also, when I speak of chasidic Judaism, I'm primarily referring to the teachings and life-style of the founder of Chasidism, the Baal Shem Tov, his disciples, and their disciples up to the present day. The term *chasid* is used throughout Jewish sacred literature in similar senses, but a discussion of this is beyond the scope of this book.

THE IMPACT OF CHASIDISM
ON TRADITIONAL JUDAISM

With this in mind, I felt it important to document the philosophical and practical results that Chasidus has contributed to the understanding of Torah. People constantly ask me, isn't Chasidus an approach for *chasidim?* Why and how does it have any relevance to me? I'm a simple Jew who studies the Talmud and does the *mitzvos,* leave this esoteric stuff to the kabbalists, or at least let me first finish leaning Talmud and then I'll take a peek into Chasidus!

My goal with this book is to demonstrate that chasidic teachings are rooted in the very essence of Torah, Talmud, Midrash, etc., and that they have brought life and enthusiasm to the study of Torah. In the past, when Jews lived in a Jewish environment, the depth and soul of Torah might have been absorbed by osmosis, while rabbis and educators focused on the legal details. Today, when science and humanistic culture dominate our society, it's imperative to take steps to explore Torah as an all-encompassing guide to life, from the most refined philosophical studies to the toys and games of little children. This is the contribution of Chasidus.

Chasidus isn't just for *chasidim* or for *tzaddikim,* it's for everyone. All it takes is the willingness and open-mindedness to allow yourself to taste this wonderful recipe and see how it makes Torah a real part of your day-to-day life.

THE PRIMARY GOAL OF THE BOOK: *BAALEI TESHUVAH*—RETURNEES TO JUDAISM

Today the *baal teshuvah* (returnee) movement is stronger than ever. Truth-seeking Jews in great numbers are considering leading a Torah life-style or have already begun to do so. In their search for direction, many have been discouraged from investigating and practicing a chasidic life-style. Some have been been told that the traditional approach, without any changes, is for them, or that chasidic Judaism is for those from a chasidic family lineage. My objective is to inform these sincere people that Chasidus is not just for one group of people. It is an alternative for everyone, including them. For those who do not want to consider themselves full-fledged *chasidim,* there are tremendous advantages in studying Chasidus and adopting those practices that are helpful and meaningful. I have written more about this in the epilogue.

WHAT'S BEING SAID, NOT WHO'S SAYING IT

It is my hope and wish that this book will be read for its content. As the Rambam says in his introduction to Tractate *Avos,* "Don't look at *who* is saying it, but at *what* is being said." If it is true and important, learn about it, internalize it! I write this book for everyone, the *chasid* and the non*chasid,* the affiliated and the nonaffiliated. However, a certain amount of experience will help in grasping its points. The more one is knowledgeable in Traditional Judaism, the more one will truly appreciate this book.

May God grant us the ability to allow our true selves to manifest themselves through the study of Chasidus. May we merit the teachings of Torah from the mouth of our righteous *Moshiach,* who will reveal to us the essence of Torah in a comprehensible way. Amen, Now!

I

THE PHILOSOPHICAL

1

Principles of Traditional Judaism

The basic principles of Torah are outlined in the Written Torah itself. The first one is found in God's words to Abraham, "so that you shall command them (the descendants of Abraham) to follow my ways" (Genesis 18:19), meaning the study of Torah and observance of the *mitzvos,* the two basic components of traditional Judaism. Without these, all else is empty. Rabbi Yosef Yitzchok Schneerson in *Hayom Yom* (9 *Nissan*) put it succinctly: "Jewish wealth is not houses and gold. The everlasting Jewish wealth is: Being Jews who keep Torah and *mitzvos,* and bringing into the world children and grandchildren who keep Torah and *mitzvos.*"

Continuing through the Torah, Exodus (3:12) clearly states that the reason God took the Jewish people out of Egypt was "in order to serve him on this mountain (Mount Sinai)," where they received the Torah. Without the giving and acceptance of the Torah, there was no reason to take the Jewish people out of slavery.

Going a little deeper, the giving of the Torah was itself a stage in the liberation from slavery, because without Torah a person is a slave. Egypt or Beverly Hills, a slave is a slave wherever he is! One becomes a free person only when one acts in a free manner. Learning Torah and doing its *mitzvos* "frees" a person from slavery to the *yetzer hara,* the "evil inclination."

GOD REWARDS US WITH OUR MATERIAL NEEDS

In the book of *Vayikra,* at the beginning of the portion *Bechukosai* (26:3ff.), the Torah says, "if you will walk in my statutes and guard my commandments, I will give you rain in its appropriate time." The Baal Shem Tov explains the verse not just to mean rain in its literal sense, but *gishmeichem* "your *gashmius,*" all physical and material needs. Everything will be provided for by God if we just follow his *mitzvos.* The Torah here enumerates the many rewards for the observance of Torah, followed by a detailed list of the punishments for the opposite. This *tochocho,* "rebuke," is difficult to swallow, but the traditional approach doesn't shy away from them, rather it acknowledges the full impact and literal meaning. Yes, one is punished for one's sins, because one is responsible for all of one's actions. There is a right and a wrong. God gave us the ability to control ourselves, and therefore, since we are capable, we are responsible. Lack of self-control leads to punishment. Tough words, but true.

The Baal Shem Tov's interpretation is supported by Traditional Judaism as stated clearly in the Mishnah and throughout our prayers. Let us go back to the concept of reward from a traditional perspective. Each morning we begin the day's study of the Oral Torah by saying a

Mishnah (*Pe'ah* 1:1) that teaches about various rewards. Some will be given to us during our lifetime, and others in the afterlife, known as *Olom Haba*. The Traditional Jew simply understands this to mean, ''I will be rewarded for doing the *mitzvos.*'' He goes forward with a solid belief in God's promise. This belief keeps him going in the right direction. The hope and anticipation that there is an afterlife, a better place with wonderful feelings and experiences, makes the practice of the *mitzvos* worthwhile.

This concept is of great importance in the mind of the Traditional Jew. This world, no matter how inconsequential it may be in the long run, nevertheless has the power to distract us from our Creator. However, physical pleasures are only temporary. Even though they satisfy for a while, the Jew is looking for an eternal bond with life, and that can only come from the spiritual. This spirituality is what makes involvement in the physical world worthwhile. Hence, the rewards promised to us by Torah are vital; without them, this life is a big waste of time!

PRAYERS THAT EMPHASIZE
REWARDS FOR FOLLOWING TORAH

This idea of reward can be found throughout the prayer service. The *Ashrei* prayer teaches the importance of sitting in God's tents and appreciating his greatness. Later in the prayer we read, ''Everyone puts their hope in you, and you sustain them: You open your hands and satiate all living creatures,'' meaning as long as a Jew puts his hope and trust in the Almighty, He will reciprocate and provide for his needs. The psalmist continues by saying, "God is close to all those who call Him." All God wants is for us to call out to Him.

Later come the *Shema* and the *V'hoya im shom-oah* prayers, both emphasizing the above concepts. First, the basic adherence to God and His command-ments, loving Him with all of one's heart, soul, and might. Then comes the study of Torah, with oneself and one's children, then the *mitzvos* of donning *tefillin* and putting up *mezuzos.* It's only after all of these that the *V'hoya* portion follows. The *V'hoya* paragraph says that following these *mitzvos* leads to reward.

Towards the conclusion of the *tefillah,* prayer ser-vice, many congregations say another psalm (86). "A prayer to David . . . guard my soul because I am a *cha-sid* . . . save your servant because I trust in you . . . be-stow grace and favor upon me because I call to you each day . . ." Clearly King Dovid gives God a reason why He should be kind and favorable towards him. He acknowl-edges that without his commitment to God as a *chasid,* and without his trust and faith in God, God won't re-spond. He realizes that God desires that he beseech Him and enumerate the reasons why he is worthy of God's grace, and that it is proper to "force God's hand," by showing clearly what one has done for Him and what rewards are deserved based on His promises in the Torah.

THE CODE OF JEWISH LAW

Traditional Judaism uses the code of Jewish law as its manual for daily living. The code has thousands of details as to how a Jew should lead his or her life. For the Traditional Jew, it's impossible to be a "good Jew" without adhering to the laws mentioned in the code.

Not only are the six hundred and thirteen *mitzvos* of paramount importance, but each and every detail that explains and clarifies the words of the Torah is just as important. In fact, without the code we wouldn't know how to implement the words of the Torah. Often, the instructions of the Torah are unclear to the human mind and eye, and along comes the Oral Torah, in the form of the code, and makes everything crystal clear.

Traditional Judaism calls the code *din,* law. *Din* contains the required laws. Matters that are good and praiseworthy, although not obligated by scriptural and rabbinical law, are called *Lifnim Mishuras Hadin,* "more than the letter of the law." They are also called *midas Chasidus,* "measuring things by the chasidic (in the general sense) yardstick."

For example, the Talmud (*Bava Kamma* 30a) says that if a person desires to act like a *chasid,* he should study all the details recorded in the Mishnah of "Ethics of the Fathers." The commentators explain that this refers to the practices and ideals of Torah which are beyond the requirements of the law. As Judaism has grown in the centuries since the Mishnah, many of the practices in the Ethics of the Fathers have been codified as an integral part of the law, while newer innovations have taken their place as "beyond the letter of the law." However, for the Traditional Jew these things are optional. The main thing is adherence to the codes. This is why the word *din* is a household word in Traditional communities and homes.

A TRADITIONAL JEW KEEPS ALL THE TRADITIONS

This approach leads a Jew to a strict adherence to Torah and its codes. As far as practice is concerned, the

Traditional Jew is committed to 100 percent of the Torah. A Traditional Jew will keep all traditions without deviating one iota. Praying three times a day isn't good enough, it has to be with a *minyan*—a quorum of ten men over the age of thirteen. Being careful what to say and what not to say is also central to the tradition. Gossip is forbidden, and idle talk is frowned upon. Sexual practices are regulated, and any deviation is considered tantamount to pagan practices. The list continues, both on the positive and negative side. The Traditional Jew doesn't reject the words of the Rabbis— he understands their importance. In fact, he realizes that without them, the words of the Torah would not be understood. He also realizes that the Rabbis who derived the codes from Torah were godly people, totally committed to the words of Torah. They were living examples of Torah and its codes.

These are the fundamental principles of Traditional Judaism. Without them, one can not call oneself a Traditional Jew. Based on this, we must enumerate the basic principles of Chasidism before we can understand the contribution of Chasidus to this already existing framework.

2

Principles of Chasidism

In addition to strict adherence to every detail of Jewish law, a *chasid* goes above and beyond the law; not just in the sense of fulfilling all that's written in Ethics of the Fathers, but also in the way he does *mitzvos* and learns Torah. To understand this better, let's focus on several key principles in Chasidism.

As mentioned in the introduction, Chasidus was revealed by the Baal Shem Tov at a period in our history when Jews were oppressed physically and spiritually. The Baal Shem Tov brought hope and strength to many Jews. One way was through emphasizing concepts which had been neglected to such an extent that it was as if he had introduced them.

First is the idea that God is the only reality. As the Torah states (*Devarim* 4:35), "There is no more besides Him." The Baal Shem elaborated on this notion based on the commentary of the Midrash *Tehillim* on the verse in Psalms (119:89), "Forever, Hashem (God), Your word stands in the heavens." He explained the Midrash to imply that there is no other existence besides existing for God.

This concept surprised world Jewry at the time, because their understanding of God and His unity didn't exclude the concept of other existences. They knew that besides God, there are no other Gods. However, as far as all other matter within the creation was concerned, since God created it, therefore He gave it strength and vigor. God created it, therefore it exists! (They did not believe, heaven forbid, that God had completely abandoned the world, an error made by some early philosophers. As explained in Rabbi Dov Ber Shneuri's *Derech Chayim, Shaar HaTeshuva,* Chapter 9, pp. 13a–b, they believed that God's supervision over these matters was so hidden as to be absolutely unrecognizable, as if the world existed independently of God.)

The Baal Shem Tov brought out that anything exists only because at that very moment God is sustaining it with his utterance. That is the meaning of "Forever, Hashem, your word stands in the heavens." If He were to remove His utterance for one instant, the whole world would return to the state it was in before the Six Days of Creation. It would be as if it had never existed. (To better understand this philosophical difference, which is based upon two ways of understanding the kabbalistic concept of *tzimtzum,* "contraction," see part two of *Tanya* [*Shaar Hayichud V'emuna*]. It is interesting to note that the successors of the Vilna Gaon eventually came around to the interpretation of Chasidus. In regard to the understanding of *tzimtzum,* in the book *Nefesh HaChaim* [*Shaar* 3, Chapter 7] by Rabbi Chaim of Volozhin, he agrees with the chasidic view. This is another example of the influence that Chasidus had on Traditional Judaism.)

DIVINE PROVIDENCE

A related teaching of the Baal Shem is that God's providence supervises every form of matter directly. Until the Baal Shem, most Jewish philosophers considered that God cared specifically for every detail of human life. However, in regard to all other domains, including the inanimate, vegetative, and animal realms, they believed that God didn't dictate their fate in detail, rather that God's "Providence" was for each species. For example, God makes sure that vegetative life will continue to exist, regardless of the fact that people are cutting down trees or doing other things to destroy the habitat. God's overall providence will not allow the total destruction of this species, but the particular details of the growth of vegetation, according to this doctrine, isn't God's concern.

The reason for this was that they felt these other forms of existence weren't important enough to justify God's dealing with them. To say that when a leaf falls off a tree, and then a wind comes along and blows it over from its right side to its left side, that this should be due to God seemed too insignificant in the overall plan of creation to warrant God's direct involvement. Then the Baal Shem came along and said that to think this way about God is inconceivable. God is truly infinite—in His eyes there is no difference between big and small. Citing Rabbi Meir ibn Gabbai (author of *Avodas Hakodesh*), he contended that if you believe God is the creator and a supreme being, then any limitation, including the limitation of exaltedness, is incompatible with His true power and existence.

These philosophic innovations paralleled the Baal Shem's approach to Jewish life. It's known how he would spend so much of his precious time traveling from city to city teaching little Jewish children the *Aleph-Beis.* He would also teach them how to make the blessings on foods, and he would share with them the importance of thanking God for everything one has in life. Many have asked why such a great *tzaddik* spent so much time with little children, who seemed inconsequential in the global picture? Wouldn't he have accomplished much more if he had spent his time with other great minds, dealing with pressing issues of a universal and cosmic nature? The answer was that just as nothing is too insignificant for God's providence, so, too, every Jew is infinitely precious. This warm approach counteracted the alienation that simple Jews had experienced because of the stress on intellectual achievement prevalent in the Jewish community.

The Baal Shem's approach to children and the simple folk was an extension of his vast knowledge of Torah. The reason he was able to commit so much time and energy to the simple, ignorant folk was precisely because he was such a Torah giant. An excellent teacher is able to convey the most intricate ideas to his students. The Baal Shem Tov, since he was such a great Talmud *chocham,* was able to communicate the inner dimensions of Torah to everyone, including the uneducated.

JUDAISM DOES NOT EQUAL
KNOWLEDGE OF TORAH AND TALMUD

This denigration of Jews who were less learned stemmed, unfortunately, from those who were learned in Talmud. Prior to the Baal Shem's arrival, the common feeling was, "If you're knowledgeable in Torah then you're a Jew, otherwise, you're not." Of course this was not meant literally, since the children of a Jewish mother are Jewish. However, the ignorant were considered second-class citizens, unworthy and despicable! They weren't called to the Torah to receive an *aliyah,* they weren't part of the social structure, and people would cross the street when they approached!

THE BAAL SHEM TOV TEACHES THAT JUDAISM EQUALS HAVING A *NESHOMAH*

What the Baal Shem Tov was doing when he spent time with the simple folk and children was demonstrating that the essence of Jews and Judaism is not accumulated knowledge but the sincerity of the heart. The first principle of Chasidism is that God is the only reality, and this perception of the unity of God, the Baal Shem explained, is present in the *neshomah,* or soul, that every Jew has.

The Baal Shem taught all of Jewry, from old to young, from scholar to ignoramus, that it is the *neshomah* that is of paramount importance and it is the *neshomah* that is the true criterion of being a Jew. Therefore, since all Jews have a *neshomah,* when a Jew allows his *neshomah* to be manifest, he actually "tastes and sees" (Psalms 34:9) God's unity as the only existence. This *neshomah* experience leads a Jew to join and unite with all Jews. This idea has been expounded upon in the book, written by the first Chabad Lubavitcher Rebbe, Rebbe Schneur Zalman of Liadi, also known as the Alter Rebbe.

Chapter 32 of the *Tanya* states that the only way possible for a person to truly unite with another person, to the extent of *ve'ahavta l're'acho komocho,* "love your friend as yourself," is through activating the *neshomah*. Otherwise, if based on the body, or even the mind, a person always has more love for himself, since he is close to his own body and mind. If one's focus is the soul, then he goes about the *mitzvah* of *Ahavas Yisroel* with truth and sincerity. What he will find is the other person's soul, enabling him to love him regardless of his faults. Furthermore, this actualizing of the *neshomah* will elevate him to his true self, so much so that he won't see faults in the other, because he will have reached a place within himself that goes beyond negativity and evil. Naturally, this will cause him to see only good in others, leading to true, unconditional love.

THE *NESHOMAH* IS A JEW'S MEASURING STICK

This idea can be better understood with a story of a chasidic rebbe called the Apter Rav, or the "Ohev Yisroel." He once asked his son to touch his hand. His son did so. He then asked his son, "What did you feel?" His son replied, "I felt your physical hand." He responded to his son, "Since you touched me with your physical hand, you felt my physical hand; if you had touched me with your *neshomah* you would have felt my hand as a spiritual thing." In other words, we view others based on the "glasses" we are wearing. If we activate our *neshomah,* then we only see the good in the other person. If we operate with our physical body, in its unrefined state, then we see other people's faults.

This idea of the activation of the *neshomah* is paramount to Chasidism. The modus operandi of the *chasid* is the *neshomah*. Every act that corresponds to Torah is based on the truth of the *neshomah,* however what is used and felt consciously by the person is the external, the physical, the body with its limitations. Chasidism, specifically Chabad Chasidism, has developed a method of study that enables one to consciously operate on a daily basis with one's *neshomah* being manifest and actually experienced. This connection with the true depths of the soul has drawn thousands of people to engage in the learning of Chasidus.

WHAT IS CHASIDUS?

The purpose of Chasidus, as a branch of Torah, is to learn how to serve God by following the principles taught by the Baal Shem Tov. Chasidus goes beyond *Mussar* (as explained in Chapter 10) in incorporating the superrational as well as the rational. Most chasidic rebbes only taught orally, while others wrote books or commentaries on other texts, especially the weekly Torah portions. Their teachings inspired the *chasidim,* even those who were not advanced in Jewish studies, to act beyond the letter of the law.

Rabbi Shneur Zalman, as the exponent of Chasidus in Lithuania, had the job of putting Chasidus into a rational form that could be studied as one studies the Talmud. As the previous Lubavitcher Rebbe explained in several essays, Chabad Chasidus is the study of divinity, using the faculties of the mind as a tool to inspire the heart and emotions, which leads to sincere and effective action. This study requires an investment of time and effort, similar to the learning of Talmud. It compares various Torah points of view in spirituality in much the same way that the Talmud compares legal theories. Just as Talmud study gives mental sharpness, enabling one to see the halachic implications in daily life, learning Chasidus can impart an ability to see and utilize the spiritual good in everything and everyone.

To recap, the second principle of Chasidism is the study of Chasidus. What follows are additional practical principles of Chasidism.

ISKAFYA—SUPPRESSING DESIRES

There is a chasidic dictum, *"vos men tor nit, tor men nit, un vos men meg, darf men nit"*—what's forbidden is forbidden, and what's allowed isn't necessary. This idea can be found in the Ramban's commentary on *Vayikra* (19:2) where he explains the verse "Holy shall you be," to teach a Jew that he must be holy in all matters. Otherwise, it is possible, according to the Ramban, to be "a *noval,* a degraded person, with the permission of the Torah." For example, he may indulge in food to the point of gluttony, based on the fact that the food is kosher and the Torah does not say exactly how much one should eat. Since he is using the Torah concept of kosher to justify his personal desires, he is called a degraded person; he is abusing the Torah.

The Hebrew word for holiness, *kadosh,* means separated. A *chasid* realizes that he doesn't have to unite himself with everything. Just because Torah says something is not forbidden doesn't automatically allow one to indulge in it. If this item will be used for a divine purpose, fine. If its use is only for self-gratification, then according to the Ramban, this violates the Torah's command "Be Holy." The *Sefer* [book] *Charedim,* (Rabbi Elazar Azkari, Venice, 1601) counts this commandment as one of the 613 *mitzvos.*

This concept is a central principle of paramount significance in chasidic philosophy. Without it, one cannot truly appreciate Chasidism. This principle is also known as *Iskafya,* suppression, to suppress the conceal-ment of God caused by nature. By withholding himself from seeking physical pleasure that is not for a godly purpose, a *chasid* demonstrates that nature is not the boss. He thus provides room for God to reveal Himself.

Simply put, to be a *chasid* one needs to practice *Iskafya.* One simple way of practicing *Iskafya* is, for example, if presented with a choice between two dif-ferent portions of a certain food, to choose the one that looks less attractive. In this small way one makes an immediate separation between what is wanted and what is needed.

In our generation, when it seems that the whole world is on a diet, the notion of *Iskafya* has developed further. The Lubavitcher Rebbe, Rabbi M. M. Schneer-son, was once asked how the students in the Yeshiva should practice *Iskafya.* He answered that when they get up from their learning to go to the dining hall, they should continue to think about what they have just learned as they are walking, instead of allowing their minds to drift. It is necessary to eat, and perhaps to eat well, but there is no need to get involved in eating as a separate sphere of existence where the presence of the Torah is not felt.

Through practices like this, Chasidism unifies life around a central purpose. Instead of the endless cycle of "working hard and playing hard," one is enabled to live a fully conscious, satisfying life.

PNIMI AND *CHITZON*—DEEP AND SUPERFICIAL

Another important theme in Chasidus is the concept known as being a *pnimi,* meaning a deep and inner person. The antonym to *pnimi* is *chitzon,* external or superficial. The *chitzon* is quick to judge, and is looking for immediate gratification. On the other hand a *pnimi* constantly strives for truth, which takes a long time to find, whether it be within or outside the self. A *pnimi* is patient and not impressed by fads and the whims of society. The *pnimi* will explore everything very carefully; he will absorb everything in a manner that leaves an indelible impression upon him.

Chasidus wants a Jew to serve God with *pnimiyus,* focused concentration. The worst possible embarrassment for a *chasid* is being called a *chitzon,* just as the highest compliment is to be called a *pnimi.*

Why isn't being called a talmudic scholar the greatest complement that a *chasid* can receive? The reason is because it's possible to be a Talmudic scholar and be a *chitzon,* and it's possible to be a *pnimi* and not be a talmudic scholar. The criteria for being a *pnimi* is not quantity of Torah knowledge, but quality of character, founded on restraint from indulgence and development of the self-abnegation known as *bittul.* A *chasid* might have a tremendous amount of knowledge in chasidic philosophy, but if he hasn't attained *bittul,* or at least aspired towards it, he is considered a *chitzonisdiker chasid,* a superficial person.

AVODAH—SERVICE

The idea of being a *pnimi* and not a *chitzon,* is associated with another important principle of Chasidus. This is the concept of *avodah,* literally meaning service (to God). This idea has been explained at length in the *Tanya,* Chapter 15. The basic idea of *avodah* is what we call effort. There are things that each of us possess that are natural. For some it's a sharp mind, for others it's a kind heart, and for others it's a streak of compassion. Are these characteristics the pinnacle of the human? Do they establish what a human being truly is? Chasidus says, not necessarily. On the contrary, it's quite possible that even while using these characteristics, a person could become stagnant and frigid. Only an individual who exercises effort in his daily life can truly experience refinement of character. Otherwise, it's not important that they have a sharp mind or a kind heart—they were born this way! God was kind and gave it to them, they didn't cause it!

On the other hand, it's possible for someone with a simple mind, or a heart that sometimes is kind and other times is not, to truly be a servant of God. That is because this person exerts effort in whatever he does, even though his actions may be simple and seemingly insignificant. This Chasidus calls *avodah*.

LIVING LIFE WITHOUT *AVODAH*
IS INHERENTLY UNHOLY

Based on this notion, we can understand a puzzling statement in chapter one of *Tanya*. Rabbi Shneur Zalman says that the "animal drive" within the human sustains the basic life force of the person. He explains this drive as being associated with the blood. However, his precise language demands clarification. He says, "One soul originates in the *klipah* and *sitra achra*, negative forces. It is this *nefesh*, soul, that is clothed in the blood of a human being, giving life to the body; as it is written, 'for the *nefesh* of the flesh is in the blood.'

From [this *nefesh*] stem all the evil characteristics, deriving from the four evil elements within it. . . .''

It seems clear that there are two distinct aspects to this *nefesh*. One is the very fact that it gives life to the body, the other, that from this *nefesh* come about evil traits. Why is the first idea of the *nefesh,* that it gives life to the body, considered *klipah*—negative? What's so bad about sustaining the existence of the body?

I heard the explanation from one of my *mashpi'im,* spiritual mentors, that the *Tanya* is teaching us that being alive without a purpose and mission as part of one's very existence is tantamount to being associated with *klipah!* A heavy statement! However, based on our previous understanding of *avodah,* it makes sense. Just because we were created by God and we are alive doesn't automatically mean that we are holy and positive.

WHAT IS NATURAL IS *KLIPAH*

On the contrary, the Alter Rebbe says several lines later that all the good traits natural to Jews, such as compassion and benevolence, come from *klipah!* Why? Because, again, one of the fundamental ideas of Chasidus is *avodah,* effort. Without it, Chasidus teaches, the finest qualities can be *klipah!* Therefore, before discussing the sinful actions caused by the "animal drive," which are clearly negative and *klipah,* the Alter Rebbe suggests that the very feeling that "I exist," that there is a will to live, can be a negative experience. Sure God created me, and sure God gives me the essential life force; however, without the purpose and effort associated with serving God, the result is *klipah.*

WHAT IS A GOOD JEW?

This idea is one of the most important discoveries of Chasidus. Until Chasidus came along, a person who learned Torah and practiced the *mitzvos* was considered not only a good Jew, but the ultimate. Then along came Chasidus, who opened the eyes of traditional Judaism and said, "Not necessarily!" Sitting and studying Torah and doing all 613 *mitzvos* does not necessarily add up to the true service of God.

Why not? Chasidus defines goodness as godliness. A good person is a godly person. Perhaps the person who fulfills Torah and *mitzvos* is doing it for very human reasons, reasons that have nothing to do with godliness. It could be that he is naturally studious and indifferent to the pleasures and temptations of this world, or that he was raised in a good home and never tempted to do otherwise, or that once upon a time he put in some effort and made studiousness and goodness his second nature. In all these cases he isn't moving. He is acting as a part of nature, not as a godly person.

This is the answer of the first Chabad Rebbe to the question of what is the purpose of Chasidus. It is the teachings of Torah that bring about a change in the nature of one's personal traits. Chabad literature makes the clear distinction between "*effecting changes in natural traits*" and "*changing the nature of personal traits.*" The first is expected from all Jews in their following of the Torah, to change any trait which contradicts the laws of the Torah, or is extreme and unmanageable, as explained in Rambam, *Hilchos Deyos.* The second is the accomplishment of Chasidus, to change the nature of all traits, including those that are good and refined, as hinted in the book of Proverbs (3:6), "in all your ways you shall know him," and in Ethics of the Fathers (2:12) that "all your deeds should be for the sake of Heaven." In this field, success isn't measured in accomplishments but in effort.

SIMCHAH—JOY

Another key principle in Chasidism is *simchah,* joy. If the reader has gotten this far he may be wondering, "How is it possible to be joyous when one is so far from the ideals of Chasidus? Maybe I should wait until I have completely subjugated my material appetites, become a deep, inward person, and transformed all of my emotions!" The answer is, that's what the *yetzer hara* wants. (The *yetzer hara,* evil inclination, uses depression as its major tool, especially among those who are Torah scholars. See Chapter 14 for an explanation.)

However, "Joy and strength are in his place" (1 Chronicles 16:27). Since success is measured by effort, every step a person makes, whether it be a good deed or the suppression of an unkind thought, is a success. Success makes a person happy, and success in *avodah* makes a person truly happy. It is only *chitzonyus,* trying to measure oneself by artificial standards, in terms of accomplishments rather than effort, that brings about guilt and depression.

King Dovid says in Psalms (100:2), *"ivdo es Hashem b'Simchah* . . . ,"* serve God with joy. The *chasid* identifies this with an all-encompassing fervor towards God in his daily life. For the *chasid,* serving God without joy is equivalent to not serving him at all. This is based on the interpretation of the holy Arizal, quoted in

Shelah, Asarah Maamarot (3:4) on the verse in *Devarim* (28:47), "Because you did not serve God your Lord with joy and gladness of the heart, from an abundance of everything [good] . . . [therefore you will serve your enemies]." The simple meaning is: "When you had an abundance of everything, you did not serve God with joy . . ." However, the Arizal interprets it thus: "You did not serve God with a joy *greater than* that caused by an abundance of everything . . ."

In other words, without the Arizal's interpretation, the verse is telling us that one needs to serve God with ordinary joy. However, the Arizal says that such ordinary joy is not enough. One needs to serve God with a joy that supersedes any possible form of joy that he would have from worldly success. Even those *mitzvos* which are done by rote, because he was brought up that way, or because he feels community pressure, or because he has a profession that necessitates a certain religious status, even these *mitzvos* can and should be suffused with joy. By bringing to them the proper intention, the desire to serve God, one takes what was lifeless and revives it. As the chasidic adage says, "transforming the cold intellect, this is the revival of the dead!" (*Hayom Yom* 11 *Sivan*). Just as after death the body becomes cold, so, too, the human intellect prior to refinement is cold and dead.

Of course, doing a *mitzvah* without feeling and *simchah* is better than not doing it at all. However, in our context, the goal is to attain a feeling of *simchah* in *avodas Hashem,* the service of God. From this perspective, *simchah* is an integral part of serving God. If *simchah* is missing, not only is it a cold and lifeless act, but in a sense it's tantamount to no performance at all.

SIMCHAH IS THE KEY
TO *DAVENING* AND LEARNING

Simchah is a fundamental element in prayer and learning. Without *simchah,* one cannot adequately serve God, because depressing thoughts and negative feelings present themselves as reality. Only through *simchah* can one truly serve God constantly.

There is another aspect to the importance of *simchah.* This is the concept of *simchah* being the springboard to going beyond ordinary limitations, whether of a physical nature or fear of what other people will think. The sages have said, *"Simchah poretz Geder,"* joy breaks through obstacles.

SIMCHAH SHATTERS BARRIERS

When *simchah poretz Geder, simchah* breaks down the barriers of convention, this, Chasidus explains, is the service of *b'chol miodecho,* "with your entire essence" (*Devarim,* 6:5). There is also a service of *b'chol livovecho,* "with your entire heart", and one of *b'chol nafshecho,* "with your entire soul" (*Devarim* 6:5). Both of these have inherent limitations. A *simchah* based on the heart and soul is limited to the feelings of the heart and the soul. No matter how great the heart and soul are, they are necessarily limited; therefore, the *simchah* resulting from these approaches is limited. On the other hand, serving God with one's entire essence goes beyond limitations, because the essence is connected to God's essence, which isn't limited to the laws of nature. The essence gives a person the power to do more than he "should" be able to according to the laws of nature, and even according to the limitations imposed by Torah. *Simchah* is the key to revealing this essence and breaking down the barriers.

For example, when one has a medical problem, it is natural to feel down. One could feel this way even if he were serving God *b'chol livovicho* and *b'chol nafshicho*. However, when a Jew activates his essence, he realizes that the illness itself came from God and is God's will. The Jew says, obviously it was given to me to draw out my inner strength. This is only possible if one activates an inner *simchah* that shatters all boundaries. This is *b'chol miodicho*.

SIMCHAH'S IMPACT ON THE FUTURE: POSITIVE THINKING

Finally, *simchah* has its impact on one's future. Not only does one serve God with joy, realizing how fortunate he is and exceeding his limitations, but *simchah* makes it possible to serve God in the midst of a negative situation, even such a situation that the Torah itself calls negative, with true joy, knowing that God will help him. The famous Chasidic adage *"tracht gut vet zein gut,"* think positive and it will indeed be positive, is the ultimate expression of *simchah*.

In other words, trust in God is a direct result of serving God with true *simchah*. Otherwise, one might not be able to serve God with joy, because he knows he has problems, not just imagined problems, but such things that the Torah calls problems. It is only through *simchah* that one is able to have trust in God and know 100 percent that it will be good, and therefore serve God with a true joy that shatters all limitations, even though he is currently hurting.

SIMCHAH—THE PEAK OF A *CHASID'S DAVENING*

This idea of *simchah* is highlighted in a *chasid*'s *tefillah,* prayer. To illustrate the point, let me share with you a story by Rabbi Shneur Zalman, who was a genius of Torah. He had studied the entire Talmud with its commentaries many times by the age of sixteen. Having exhausted all the lesser teachers, he had a choice between the great lights of his generation. His choice was between traveling to Vilna and spending time with the great Gaon, Reb Eliyahu, or going to Mezritch to study with the successor of the Baal Shem Tov, the Maggid, Reb Dov Ber. Reb Shneur Zalman resolved his dilemma by saying, "I've been learning Torah all my life and I know how to learn, however, what it means to commune with God, to serve God through prayer, this I am lacking. Therefore I will travel to Mezritch, where Reb Dov Ber is teaching the importance of uniting with God through *davening,* prayer."

MEZRITCHER MAGGID AND VILNA GAON: *DAVENING* VERSUS LEARNING

It was prayer that made Reb Shneur Zalman choose Mezritch over Vilna. Of course the Vilna Gaon *davened,* and surely his *davening* was with great concentration. However, it was a means to an end. Since there was an obligation to pray, so he prayed; however, his goal in life was the study of Torah. His *davening* was a Torah-oriented *davening,* meaning that his focus was the learning that followed his *davening.* To quote Rabbi Berel Wein, who records the life and history of the Vilna Gaon in his book *Triumph of Survival* (p. 100–107),

"The preservation of the priority of Torah scholarship as the focal point of Jewish life was thus perhaps his (the Vilna Gaon's) greatest achievement."

In Mezritch the *davening* was an end in itself. This Reb Shneur Zalman had never experienced. What makes a *chasid*'s *davening* special? It's the element of *simchah,* also called *chayos* and *hislahavus,* fervor and enthusiasm.

This *chayos* in *davening* doesn't necessarily manifest itself in clapping with the hands or shaking back and forth, although some chasidic groups, such as *Bratzlov* and *Karlin,* require outward gestures. The focal point is a deep inner sense of joy that permeates every fiber of one's being. For example, when an artist looks at a beautiful painting, he doesn't scream or dance out of excitement. Rather, he is absorbed by the painting to the point that he is "glued." If someone touches him, he doesn't feel it, because he is not there. He has been taken away by the painting to another realm. Yet, he doesn't get excited and emotional, rather he is very quiet and passive. This Chasidus calls *deveikus,* complete attachment that comes from the most inner core of the person. In the same vein, one who davens with great *deveikus* is completely absorbed by the prayers to the point that, for him, the only thing that exists is God.

This is the ultimate quality of *davening* with *simchah* and *chayos.* Chasidic *davening,* with its preparations, is the practical, day-to-day effort to bridge the gap between two sayings of our sages, "One cannot begin to *daven* without seriousness" and "One cannot begin to daven without joy" (*Brochos* 30b, 31a).

To better understand what *davening* is from a chasidic perspective, and what the practical result of the Vilna Gaon's approach is, read Chapter 11 on *tefillah.*

REBBE

All these principles are based on one big principle, that the chasid has a rebbe. This will be discussed at great length in Chapter 21. However, I'll just briefly mention it here to conclude the principles of Chasidism. A rebbe, first of all, is an exceptional human being. The first step in accepting a rebbe is to realize that he is not cut from the same cloth as an ordinary Jew. This itself requires humility and leads to more humility, but it derives from fundamental principles of traditional Judaism. The ethics of the Fathers cautions that the "awe for one's teacher should be like the awe of Heaven." When one experiences a rebbe, whether through his physical presence or through his Torah, this dictum becomes more than an arbitrary rule. When one experiences the rebbe's own absolute humility toward God, one can become a totally different person.

A rebbe, in the fullest sense, is the equivalent of Moshe Rabbeinu and King Dovid. A rebbe gives inspiration, guidance, counsel, and rebuke when necessary. A rebbe and *chasidim* are one. It is impossible to be a *chasid* without a rebbe and it's impossible to be a rebbe without *chasidim*. The Baal Shem Tov was the rebbe of all existing rebbes. A Gaon, a *tzaddik,* a leader; these phrases do not begin to describe what he was. The proof is that his disciples have taken all these qualities from him.

With this enumeration of the basic components of Traditional Judaism and Chasidism, we can proceed to look at various intellectual and practical *mitzvos* with an eye to the contribution of Chasidus within the framework of Torah.

II

THE IDEOLOGICAL
CONTRIBUTION
OF CHASIDUS
WITHIN TORAH

3

Emunah, Faith

How does Traditional Judaism view the concept of faith in God? Let's talk about the thirteen articles of faith, recited daily in many congregations around the globe. These articles outline a Jew's basic commitment to God Almighty, everywhere and anywhere. Without belief in God, one cannot begin pondering the details mentioned in the articles. Prior to dealing with the specifics, one must have a 100 percent belief in God. For the Traditional Jew, belief in God means knowing that He controls everything, and accepting His judgments to be true, regardless of whether we think the result is positive or negative.

GAM ZU LITOVA—EVERYTHING IS FOR THE GOOD

For the Traditional Jew, everything that happens in life, personally and communally, is from God. Nothing happens outside of God's control, or against God's wishes. Whether it's winning the lottery or suffering afflictions, it's all from God. The Traditional Jew will not accept a God who is in the image of his own needs and desires. Rather, the Traditional Jew will say *gam zu litova,* this is also for the good, and will even make a blessing, "blessed be the truthful Judge."

What remains a mystery from a Traditional Jewish perspective is where this tremendous faith comes from. True, faith in God is the basis for our belief in Torah, however the code of Jewish law doesn't discuss the origins of this faith. Rather, this is the way it is, and that's that! (As they would say in the cheder when a child would ask a profound question, *"Ven du vest veren elter, vest du farbstein,"* when you get older, you'll understand. This response was equivalent to saying, "Don't ask that question, because you're not going to get an answer, and all you'll do by asking is confuse yourself more.") Even those *seforim,* holy books, that do delve into the topic, fall short in addressing the vital issue of how to develop and sustain one's faith.

There is a second question, equally important, and that is the question of whether or not faith in God must permeate all parts of the person. Great Jewish minds have, in effect, said yes and no. Yes, to that part of our beings that can relate to faith, and no, to that part of us that uses intellect as its guide. Intellect and faith don't mesh, is their contention. However, Chasidus reexamines the entire notion of faith, and through a deeper understanding of what *emuna* truly is, makes it possible to develop a stronger faith in God. This faith will not just impact his actions, but will influence his mind and heart as well.

EVERY JEW BELIEVES

The Jewish people are called "believers the children of believers" (*Bamidbar Rabbah* 7), they possess a natural, inherent belief in God. Wonderful. However, we see that when a robber is standing on the threshold about to gain entry into a property, he calls out to God for help! It seems rather strange. He is about to rob, which is against God's will, and yet before he commits his crime he asks God to help him! Is he normal or does he have a split personality? Chasidus says he is normal. He definitely has a belief in God, yet he has not defined to himself what it means to say, "I believe in God." He has not committed himself to understanding and perceiving what "God" represents, and even less to living in accordance with that understanding. Since he hasn't developed his belief to the point that it permeates every fiber of his being, he acts with his natural, unrefined drive. This natural drive is called by Chasidus the *nefesh habahamis,* the animalistic soul, or in talmudic terminology, the *yetzer hara,* the evil inclination, which acts on instinct, like an animal, without discerning between good and evil.

The seemingly paradoxical state of mind that this person finds himself in is perfectly normal. As Reb Shneur Zalman explains in *Tanya,* Chapter 28, there are the two sides to the Jew. One side is expressing the godly soul-drive, and the other side is expressing the animal-like soul-drive. Inner conflict is thus a sign that a Jew is healthy and normal.

EVEN A ROBBER BELIEVES

So too, Chasidus says, is the case with the robber. When the robber asks God to assist him in his venture, he is expressing his encompassing belief in God. However, what the robber hasn't developed yet is the deeper belief in God known as the essence of the *neshomah,* or the *etzem.* When a Jew awakens his *etzem,* it's impossible for him to commit an act that's contrary to God, because the *etzem* is that divine part of God within, as it is stated in *Tanya,* Chapter 2. So how is it possible for a Jew to commit an act that's contrary to God's will? It's only because he is operating with the part of the *neshomah* that's not the essential part but rather the external part. However, as far as his faith is concerned, it is complete.

HAVING *MESIRAS NEFESH* IN A FREE SOCIETY

In the discourse *"V'atoh Tetzaveh,"* 1981 (distributed by *Purim Katan,* 1992), the Lubavitcher Rebbe, M. M. Schneerson, explains that this essence has to manifest itself in every detail of a Jew's life. Even if a Jew is faced with a do or die situation and is willing to give his life for God, this still doesn't prove that he is truly living with his essence. The proof is that there were people who risked their lives to live Jewishly in Russia, but when they came to a free society, they didn't have nearly as much dedication to Judaism. Why? Because their commitment, even in Russia, was limited to that part of the *neshomah* that's stimulated and motivated by the do or die challenge. It was dependent on circumstances, albeit of a negative nature. It thrived on adversity and was able to overcome all opposition.

However, the deep essence that goes beyond the do or die ultimatum was not activated. The Rebbe says the proof of this is the fact that, in a free society, they failed the test and didn't act with the same enthusiasm. The true essence of the soul is expressed without *any* outside influences. For example, it's a Tuesday morning and a Jew is lying in bed, it's warm and cozy. Will he get up immediately and be early for his regular morning services, or continue lying there, enjoying his comfort, snoozing just a little longer and come in late, *davening* fast to catch up?

This is the test of living a life permeated with the essence of the soul. In other words, the question that one must ask oneself is, "What does my simple, mundane, day-to-day life look like?" So the ultimate objective is a total expression of the *neshomah,* regardless of history and environment, whether in Russia under pressure or in America with material wealth and as much freedom as has ever existed in our long exile.

SEEING GOD AND BEING LIKE GOD

The Rebbe says this level of *neshomah* is even greater than seeing godliness, because even though "seeing is believing," what is seen is something outside the self. The one who sees and the object that is seen are two distinct objects that are joined together. It is an *acquisition,* of the strongest kind, but still an added thing. However, it's still not *you,* it was added to you. The level of *neshomah* that is truly the essence of the Jew is the faith in God that is not called "seeing God" but rather "being like God." This is the way Chasidus understands the concept of faith. It is all-encompassing, penetrating one's inner core, and causing a behavior that's consistent with God's will.

This idea has been explained in chapter 18 of the *Tanya*. Reb Shneur Zalman explains that even a *kal shb'kalim,* someone who is extremely easy on himself and doesn't practice God's *mitzvos,* when faced with a challenge to his faith in God will give up his life rather than do anything that contradicts that faith. The question is, how is this possible? As far as his behavior is concerned, he isn't fulfilling God's Torah, he isn't putting on *tefillin,* or eating kosher, and yet when challenged he comes through for God! Chasidus explains that the reason he is able to do this isn't because he comes through for God; rather he comes through for himself, because he activates his true self, which is a part of God. At that point he doesn't have a desire not to be himself. That would be insane, which he surely is not!

What this means is that even though in practice this individual isn't doing all of Torah and *mitzvos,* yet as far as his commitment and loyalty is concerned, he is bound to God. The deeper reason is that he realizes that he is part of God.

HOLISTIC HEALING: AN EXAMPLE OF A JEW'S INHERENT FAITH IN GOD

With this in mind, we can answer the two questions at the beginning of the chapter. First, what is the origin of faith? Second, does faith have to permeate every aspect of life? The chasidic view of faith in God is that this is the true person and everything else in his life, including his behavior, is the external part. Even when everything seems to be going fine, when godliness is opaque and there is no direct experience of God due to the exile, the Jew realizes that the primary thing is not there. This realization not only activates the essence of the Jew, but it eventually impacts the five senses and the mind, completely transforming them.

It's analogous to the body healing itself without the use of medicine. Holistic medicine professes to heal by allowing the body to be its natural self. Yes it takes time, however there are no risks of side effects or of the body habituating itself to drugs. The same is true in the moral sphere. When the *neshomah* is manifest, it impacts the rational self without any difficulties. If a Jew allows his *neshomah* to reveal itself, he doesn't need any outside stimuli such as praise or blame to come to realize his true identity.

A JEW IS ALWAYS CONNECTED TO GOD

This concept is addressed in the chasidic adage *"Ah Yid nisht er vill un nisht er ken zich upreisen fon getlichkeit,"* a Jew can neither willingly nor unwillingly be separated from godliness. Literally translated, a Jew doesn't want to and isn't able to tear himself away from God. This seems to be true, because to say a Jew isn't able to separate himself from God makes sense based on a Jew's inherent connection to God, as explained before. However, in regard to the statement "He doesn't want to separate himself," that seems not to be true. Even someone who is fully committed to Judaism may occasionally have *mitzvos* he does not particularly want to do.

THE TRUE WILL OF A JEW IS TO DO GOD'S WILL: THE RAMBAM'S RULING

The answer to this is found in a traditional source. The Rambam, in the laws of divorce (2:20 end), states explicitly that the true will of a Jew is to do God's will. The context is as follows. Even though, in Jewish law, the husband must originate a divorce, in certain cases, such as maltreatment, the court is authorized to force him to do so, even if he objects. The catch here is that a *get,* divorce bill, given under duress is invalid. The husband must give the *get* of his own free will. The solution to this dilemma, says the Rambam, is for the officers of the court to force him, with physical pressure if need be, until he says "I am willing."

What is going on here!? If he has to be forced, how is he willing, and if he is willing, why does he have to be forced? The Rambam heads off this objection by explaining that it is the true will of every Jew to follow the laws of the Torah. At certain times his evil inclination may influence him not to, and the force exerted by the court serves only to free him from this compulsion and enable him to reveal his true will.

As with so many concepts in Chasidus which look radical at first glance, it is possible to find traditional sources which state the germ of the idea in a form that looks even more radical. The advantage of Chasidus is that it explains these seemingly exceptional statements in a way that the intellect can grasp. Chasidus provides a path to revealing one's true, godly will.

CHASIDIC MEDITATION

How does one accomplish the manifestation of one's true essence? It is through contemplation of godly concepts in relation to one's life. The idea of the greatness of the Jewish soul is worth thinking about some more.

(In addition to giving one strength to fulfill the *mitzvos,* it can bring about a new dimension in one's love of
a fellow Jew, which, as Rabbi Akiva said, is a "great
general principle of the Torah.")

The details of this meditation are set forth in Chapters 24 and 25 of *Tanya.* Briefly, every *mitzvah* binds a
Jew to God, as indicated by the word *mitzvah,* meaning
connection. Every sin, *averah,* separates a Jew from
God, as reflected in the word *averah,* meaning transfer
(away from the realm of godliness). Therefore, when a
Jew fulfills God's *mitzvos,* he unites himself with God,
which causes unity. However, when a Jew commits a
sin, he severs his relationship, thereby causing dishar-
mony. In effect, he is asserting that God's will and his
personal will are two separate entities. This is like idolatry, whose root is the giving of importance to something outside of God.

When a Jew contemplates the above, he realizes
the importance of doing all *mitzvos* and not doing any
averah, big or small. This meditation enables one's
holy and positive feelings to control one's daily life,
thus manifesting the *neshomah.*

Another extremely powerful meditation is to realize that one is still in exile, that no matter how good
things may be, the *Bais HaMikdash,* in which everyone
was able to see ten revealed miracles, is simply not here.
Even if one's own soul is full of light, the fact that there
is still room in the world for denial of God shows that
more light is needed. Paradoxically, by realizing the lack
of this highest, messianic revelation, a Jew connects
himself to it. He derives the courage not to be satisfied
with the status quo, which has always been the greatest
motivator of human endeavors.

These thoughts are just a few among the many that can bring about a total paradigm shift, a new liveliness in Torah and *mitzvos*. The ideas are there in Traditional Judaism. Chasidus points them out and reveals their godly power. It thus brings the *emunah,* faith, into all spheres of life, starting with the intellect.

4

Mitzvos: Chukim, Mishpotim, and Eduyos—Statutes, Laws, and Testimonies

Mitzvos are divided by the Torah into general categories. The Torah in the book of *Vayikra* (18:4) teaches us that there are *chukim* and *mishpotim*, statutes and laws. Statutes are those commandments that God has instructed us to perform without question, since their reason is unknown. *Mishpotim* are those precepts whose reason can be understood by human intelligence. The Rambam in his "Eight Chapters" (chapter 6) calls *mishpotim, mitzvos sichliyos*, rational *mitzvos*, and *chukim, mitzvos shmiyos, mitzvos* which are heard, meaning they are followed without comprehension.

In more detail, the commentators on *Devarim* (6:20) explain that there are three groups of *mitzvos*, since the category of *mitzvos sichliyos* has two subgroups. *Mishpotim* are those *mitzvos* that human rationality requires, such as the prohibition of stealing. Even if people did not derive them from pure reason, they could use their reason to learn them from animals. The

41

Talmud states (*Eruvin* 100b) that if Torah had not been given, we would learn modesty from the cat, who eliminates in private, and integrity from the ants, who do not take each other's food. These *mitzvos* are rational—the Torah does not need to command them. Then there are *eduyos*, testimonies, *mitzvos* that are reminders of a historic event, such as the *mitzvos* of Pesach, Sukkos, and *Shabbos*. Once Torah teaches us to appreciate the significance of the event, we can understand how it is important to commemorate it. The third group are the *chukim*, God's decrees which seem to have nothing to do with reason.

TRADITIONAL APPROACH TO *MITZVOS*

In the traditional approach to *mitzvos*, this division has substantial practical consequences. *Mishpotim* and *eduyos* require the involvement of the rational faculties. As the Rambam explains in his "Eight Chapters" (Chapter 6), in regard to logical *mitzvos*, positive and negative, a person who fulfills the logical *mitzvos* out of pure obedience is acting inappropriately. Since these *mitzvos* are logical, to fulfill them without the usage of logic is denying the rationality granted by God. Eventually it could lead to a corrupted character, since the person is acting on the assumption that his mind is basically irrational and desires evil.

Since, in reality, God gave us a mind, we have an obligation to Him and to ourselves to use it. Those *mitzvos* that are self-understood must be performed through understanding them. *Chukim* are very different. Their fulfillment must be only because God said so; no human logic can explain them. Put another way, *chukim* subdue and put aside the human mind, by demanding its allegiance to a power higher than itself.

EGO AND SELFLESSNESS

What is the function of these differences with regard to the human character? The impact of the *mishpotim* and *eduyos* is to reinforce and strengthen the *metzius,* existence of a person, referring not to the arrogant ego but to the healthy self. On the other hand, performance of *chukim* humbles the ego and causes *bittul,* humility. Both *metzius* and *bittul,* self-worth and humility, are essential in the healthy development of the Jew in serving God. Therefore, God chose these two general categories of *mitzvos,* to build character, or in the words of Maimonides, *"letzaref es habriyos,"* to refine people. But is this the whole story?

From a traditional perspective, *chukim* have a reason, it's just that we humans don't understand the reason. The Rambam, at the end of the laws of *meila,* misappropriation of sacred property, states that statutes are those *mitzvos* whose reason is unknown to us, clearly implying that there is a reason, but it is unknown. The same position is taken by the Ramban in his commentary on *Vayikra* 19:19. The Ramban writes that *chukim* are laws that the king has decreed without notifying his subjects of the reason. However, the king himself knows the underlying reason. Based on these commentators and others, the traditional viewpoint holds that *chukim* do have a reason; however, *we* don't know the reason because we haven't been told.

The Rambam states that a person should fulfill this type of *mitzvah* only because God decreed them. Why, if *mitzvos* do indeed have some higher explanation, does the Rambam allow only this motivation? Why not fulfill them on the basis that they inherently make sense, only it is on a level of understanding far beyond ours, and that if God granted us more brains we might merit knowing the reasons? Chasidus enlightens this issue through a deeper understanding of *chukim, mishpotim,* and *edus.*

CHUKEI RETZONECHO—
THE STATUTES OF YOUR WILL

There is a chasidic discourse from the previous Lubavitcher Rebbe, (printed in his book of discourses, 1941, p. 59) in which he analyzes the terminology of the special Chanukah prayer, *Al Hanisim.* Describing the decree of the Hellenists against the Jewish people, the exact language in the Hebrew is, *"ulehavirom mechukei retzonecho,"* "and to remove them from the statutes *(chukim)* of Your will." The Rebbe explains that the intent of the Hellenists was to eliminate the *chukim,* but not the *mishpotim* and *eduyos,* but what remains unclear is the apparent redundancy. What is the need for the word *retzonecho,* Your will? The prayer could have read *"ulehavirom mechukecho,"* "and to remove them from Your statutes," and that would have been sufficient.

THE HELLENISTS OPPOSED "YOUR [GOD'S] WILL,"
NOT ORDINARY *CHUKIM*

In regard to this question, the Lubavitcher Rebbe adds new depth. The Hellenists didn't mind the fulfillment of *chukim,* as long as they had some kind of explanation, on any level, whether allegorical, moralistic, or mystical. What they couldn't stand was the fulfillment of *mitzvos* only because God said so. Their rationality could not tolerate something that claimed to transcend reason, based only on "Your will." It was the absolute holiness and divinity of the *chukim* that they opposed.

In other words, the Hellenists agreed to the concept of *mitzvos* as a proper tool for human refinement. They appreciated the great insight that could be gleaned from them, but they couldn't fathom a Jew doing a *mitzvah* only because God said so and for no other reason, even an esoteric one. This "unacceptable" relationship to *mitzvos* is known as *kabbalas ol,* accepting the yoke of heaven. The only reason for the *mitzvah* is because God says so; everything else detracts from its purity and holiness.

TORAH SOURCES FOR DEEPER MEANING OF *CHUKIM*

This notion of *chukim* being totally beyond logic has support from the fundamental commentator on the Torah and Talmud, Rashi. On *Yoma* 67b, Rashi elucidates the word *chukah,* it is only a decree of the king. In the Torah, Rashi comments on *Bereishis* (26:5), *Shemos* (15:26), and *Vayikra* (19:19) that a *chukah* is the "decree of the king and has no reason whatsoever." We also find in the *sefer Arvei Nachal,* from the same author as the *sefer Livushei Serod,* which is a commentary on the Code of Jewish law, in the portion on *chukas,* that all *mitzvos* are the divine will and, therefore, transcend logic. He implies that, fundamentally, *all mitzvos* are *chukim*.

What about *mishpotim* and *Edus?* What is the view of Chasidus in regard to their fulfillment? Rabbi Menachem Mendel Schneerson, in *Likutei Sichos* (vol. 3, p. 898), answers this question by taking a deeper look at a *mitzvah* the Torah itself calls a *chuka,* the *parah aduma,* red heifer.

The Midrash *Tanchuma* on *Koheleth* (7:23) teaches that King Shlomo said, in regard to the red heifer, "I thought I'll be able to fathom God's wisdom, and yet I realize that His wisdom is distant from me." The simple reason Shlomo was not able to understand this particular *chukah* is that it is paradoxical: on the one hand, the person who sprinkles becomes impure, and on the other hand, the person who is being sprinkled on becomes pure! Therefore, the wisest of all humans said, "This one I can't relate to," because its details contradict each other. Since those of the other *chukim* don't, Shlomo could fathom the reasons for them.

From this Midrash we see that within *chukim* themselves there are levels, and also that the difference between *chukim* in general and the *chukah* of the red heifer is that all the other *chukim* aren't paradoxical, but *para aduma* is.

CHUKAS HAPARA—THE ESSENCE OF TORAH

Based on this, we can understand why *parah aduma* is called in the Torah, the *chukah* of the Torah. Seemingly it should be called the *chukah* of *parah adumah,* just as the Pascal sacrifice is called *chukas haPesach!*

The Alter Rebbe, in *Likutei Torah,* at the beginning of the portion of *chukas,* explains that this *chukah* in particular contains a general principle which underlies not only the other *chukim,* but every *mitzvah* of the Torah, including those that have a straightforward, logical explanation.

What is the similarity? After all, *mishpotim* and *Edus* are rational, and *chukim* are illogical. Chasidus says that the truth of the matter is that even *mishpotim* and *Edus* are essentially nonlogical. Their origin transcends logic, and since God created logic, He is not governed by it. Thus, in the last analysis, the only reason a Jew should fulfill any *mitzvah* is that God commands it. The phrase in any blessing upon a *mitzvah* is, *"asher kidishonu b'mitzvosov vtzivonu,"* "He has sanctified us with his *mitzvos* and has commanded us." This text is standard for all Jews, whether chasidic or Traditional.

MITZVAH MEANS CONNECTION WITH GOD

What does the text teach? That the only reason for doing the *mitzvah* is because God commanded us, *vtzivonu.* This is the underlying theme of all the *mitzvos.* However, in regard to *mishpotim* and *Edus,* God wanted the rational mind to be involved and excited about the particular *mitzvah.* On the other hand, in regard to *chukim,* God didn't desire that a person's mind be involved—he should fulfill the *chukah* with pure unadulterated faith. In all cases the point of initiation for all *mitzvos* is *vtzivonu,* God commands us, and ultimately that is the reason why we apply the mind. It all comes from His commandment.

SERVANT AND KING

Why does God want the essence of all *mitzvos* to be *chukim*? Ramban explains on *Devarim* 6:13, that "and you shall serve Him" means to heed all His commandments just as a servant heeds the commandments of his master. A true servant listens to his master's every wish, fulfilling them to the minutest detail, for the sole reason that his master has so commanded.

To operate from his own motives, even from a rational explanation of why his master's command is a good one, would detract. His service would not be an expression of subjugation and obedience, merely an expression of his own self. Since he understands and appreciates the greatness of his master, therefore he decides that it's more important to serve his master than to do other things. This servant is no longer dedicated totally to his master. On the contrary, his concern is for his own advancement. He feels he will become great by association. He is trading one personal desire for another.

Therefore, every *mitzvah* has as its underlying philosophy the concept of *vtzivonu*—doing *mitzvos* only because God has commanded them. When the Torah demands *avodas Hashem,* serving God, it refers to the service of the completely dedicated servant, who has no desire of his own. This is true service to God.

This essential explanation, with which Chasidus has enlightened us, shows that the foundation of all *mitzvos,* including *mishpotim* and *eduyos,* is God's command, and upon this foundation everything must stand. Together with this, it is true that the "building" of *mishpotim* and *eduyos* is made of rational, understandable materials, and this is what gives them their distinctive character.

The basic difference between the traditional and chasidic view can be summed up by an old saying of *chasidim:* ''The world (Jewish Traditional view) says, we hope *(halivai)* that we will fulfill *chukim* like we fulfill *mishpotim*—Chasidus says, just the opposite. That the truth of the matter is, we hope that we will fulfill *mishpotim* like *chukim.''*

5

Human Perfection

What is the traditional view of human perfection? Is it possible? How are we to understand mortality? Didn't Moshe Rabbeinu and King Dovid make mistakes? Weren't they blamed and punished by God? The traditional answer to these questions is, at best, acceptable. It goes something like this: Since God is our creator and we are His creatures, that very fact establishes our humanity and mortality. The logic is simple; since we were created, we have a beginning and an end—we came from somewhere and we're going somewhere. Based on this, it is impossible to be perfect.

THE JEW IS THE FIFTH DIMENSION OF CREATION

Chasidus agrees to this in general, but not with regard to the Jewish people. The *Sefer Yetzirah* states that the Jewish Nation is a fifth dimension within the creation.

51

God created four realms: the inanimate, the vegetative, the (living) animal, and the human. Then there is a fifth realm, the Jewish people.

Chasidus derives from this that the Jewish people are in essence a paradox. Even though they are a fifth dimension that is above and beyond creation, at the very same time they express this special quality in the world, the domain of the other four realms. This remarkable combination, something that is beyond time and space and yet is present within time and space, is only within the power of God Almighty.

We find a similar concept in the morning blessing, *asher yotzar*, which concludes with the words, "Blessed be God who heals all flesh and performs wonderful acts." Chasidus says that this refers to the union of the soul and the body. Even though they are opposites, God brings them together. This is wondrous and totally beyond human capability. Therefore we acknowledge this by thanking God for making the impossible to be possible. The existence of the Jewish people within creation is similarly wondrous.

Human beings possess speech and reason, but their natural imperfection and mortality is like that of the other creations. Earth erodes, plants wither, and animals die. Human beings likewise deteriorate and pass on. From this perspective one could say that whether it's Moshe Rabbeinu, King Dovid, or any ordinary person, all are human and it's impossible to be perfect. But God created the Jewish soul, which is different from those of all other creatures. For the Jewish people, as a fifth element within creation, it's not just possible, but practical to reach a godly perfection within the limited and finite world.

WITHIN CREATION AND
TRANSCENDING CREATION

The *neshomah* is an actual part of God. Therefore, the Jews are capable of transcending human frailty and imperfection. Just as God has no limitations, those who possess the *neshomah* have the ability to go beyond the boundaries of time and space. This implies that the Jewish people are, in a sense, just like God, creators!

BEING A PARTNER WITH GOD

We find support for this concept in the Talmud Tractate *Shabbos* (119b). The Talmud states that whoever recites the *vayechulu* (prayer describing God creating the world in six days, and resting on *Shabbos*) becomes a partner with God in creation. The commentator Maharsha explains that in saying this passage, the Jewish people testify that God created the world in six days and rested on *Shabbos,* and this acknowledgment is equivalent to creating the world. Thus, the person saying this becomes a partner with God in creation!

The Lubavitcher Rebbe, Rabbi M. M. Schneerson, asks a simple question: Why does one's recognition that God created the world make him or her a partner? No one has created anything, they have just proclaimed a well-known fact! True, it's a great thing, but to say that they become God's partner would mean that they have something in common with God, the Creator! This is seemingly blasphemous, God *creates* the world and the Jew only *proclaims* Him to be the creator.

In a true partnership, both parties share all aspects: profit and loss, investments, loans, etc. If there is an area in which they aren't equal, then it's not a complete partnership. To say that the Jews are God's partners would mean that they have the quality of being creators!

Chasidus explains the talmudic statement and says, yes, the Jews are real partners because they have a power of creation. This is the essence of the *neshomah,* that it is an actual part of God. What does the *neshomah* create? Chasidus explains (see *Tanya,* Chapter 6) that since the physical world is completely dominated by negative energy, on its own accord it has no power to rise above this negativity.

CREATING SOMETHING FROM NOTHING

However, a Jew was created by God with the ability to accomplish a total transformation within the world, and that amounts to creating something from nothing. When a Jew takes physical matter and incorporates it into the service of God, this is actually similar to creating *yesh miaiyin,* something from nothing. The nothing is the negative energy that's all around us, and the something is the revelation of God's unity, which is totally positive. This accomplishment is the same as God's in creating the world. There was nothing here and He made something. So, too, the Jewish people create something out of a nothing, transforming negativity to positivity.

With this in mind, it makes sense to say that the Jew is a partner. When a Jew testifies to God's creation, he or she is not just saying a prayer, but attesting to the quality of the God-given *neshomah*. This attribute makes the Jewish people the sole entity within the universe with the responsibility and obligation to create, that is to say, to transform the rest of creation. Doing this, they are full partners.

HUMAN PERFECTION REVISITED

Based on this, let us return to the concept of human perfection. Can a human being be perfect? The answer is no. Can a Jew be perfect? The answer is yes. Jewish perfection is not that one lives forever; rather, it means the perfect expression of the *neshomah*. The *neshomah* is definitely perfect, but it is up to the individual to allow it to manifest itself.

OUR JEWISH LEADERS MOSHE AND DOVID WERE PERFECT

This notion has its practical ramifications. Chasidus believes that people like Moshe Rabbeinu and King Dovid were, from a Jewish perspective, perfect. They completely transformed themselves and elevated their environment. Their imperfection was relative; they could and should have been even better. Chasidus brings a proof from 1 Kings 1:21, "you and he were missing from the table." In this verse, the Hebrew word meaning missing is *chatoim*. This word also means sinning, but for *tzaddikim,* not achieving their full potential is also called *chatoim*. On their level there is no actual sin, but there can be deficiency. Relative to their level, it is called "sin."

A *TZADDIK* FROM A CHABAD PERSPECTIVE

Rabbi Schneur Zalman, in the *Tanya,* chapters 10 and 12, defines the true *tzaddik,* based on sources in Mishnah, Talmud, and *Zohar.* A person who has never sinned and will never sin in his life is only called a *benoni,* or intermediate person, because he is still able to desire what is forbidden. The true *tzaddik* is unable even to desire a sin. However, since a *tzaddik* lives in this world, he is in a struggle with the limitations of this world to do even more good. On his level, the notion of sin is his failure to be even better.

Such an event as Moshe Rabbeinu hitting the rock rather than talking to it, as requested by God, is considered a sin for Moshe. Moshe, being who he was, should not have hit the rock but rather spoken to it. But, Chasidus contends, in no way, shape, or form did Moshe, our teacher and leader, commit a sin in the ordinary sense.

The same reasoning is true in regard to King Dovid and all other *tzaddikim.* As the Talmud says, "Whoever says that King Dovid sinned, is making a mistake." Chasidus begins with the unwavering premise that each and every *tzaddik* were godly people, whose only desire in life was to cleave to God and fulfill His will. Had they been ordinary, worldly folks, who just happened to enjoy Torah and *mitzvos* more than the average, there would have been no reason to follow them with complete faith throughout the centuries.

The Torah calls the Jewish people a "wise and understanding people!" How can we consider ourselves smart, yet follow those who are not much better than ourselves? The explanation is that these people were, compared to us, perfect. Therefore, the Torah demands that the Jewish people follow the words of these prophets and sages, notwithstanding that, at times, they could have been better and more perfect.

RUNNING TO GET YOUR REBBE'S SINS!

There is a story about Reb Naftoli of Ropshitz and his rebbe, Reb Mendel Riminover. On Rosh Hashanah, after the *Tashlich* ceremony, Reb Mendel was returning from the river. He noticed his student, Reb Naftoli, running toward him, and asked him in bewilderment, "Where and why are you running?" Reb Naftoli responded, "Rebbe, I'm running to get the sins that you just threw into the river!" This episode describes the Chasidic view of a *tzaddik*. To Reb Naftoli, his rebbe's sins were actually *mitzvos!* He couldn't imagine his rebbe having actual sins.

Did he not know that his rebbe was human? Absolutely. However, he realized that his humanity was only his physical being. With regard to his soul as it impacts the body, he knew that his rebbe was perfect. Therefore, he ran to pick up his "sins."

This concept, says Chasidus, is tangible for each and every Jew. As is said prior to reading the Ethics of the Fathers, "And your people are all *tzaddikim,*" every Jew can relate to the perfection of the *tzaddikim* because God has given him a *neshomah,* which grants the ability to rise above the limitations of humanity.

ELIYAHU AND IMMORTALITY

Another event in Jewish history reminds us of immortality from a Jewish perspective. The second book of

Kings describes the last days of the great prophet Eliyahu. Eliyahu was the one who stood at Mount Chorev and learned that God is not in the whirlwind or in the earthquake or in the fire, but rather in the still, small voice that speaks within the human soul. And it was after that vision that Eliyahu spread his coat over the person who was to become his disciple—the prophet Elisha.

The moment comes when Eliyahu is about to be taken from the world. He knows it. Elisha knows it. Eliyahu says to Elisha, "Stay here, I have to cross the Jordan. God has called on me to make that final journey at the end of my life. I am about to take the one journey that each of us must make alone."

And Elisha refuses to be separated from his rav, from his rebbe, his teacher. He says, "By the life of God and by your life, I will not leave you." The two of them walk together. As they cross the Jordan, Eliyahu says to Elisha, "Tell me what I can do for you before I am taken from you and from this life." He asks one thing: "Please grant me a double portion of your spirit." Just as Moshe, commanded by God to lay one hand on Yehoshua, his successor, instead—out of love for his student—laid on both hands, giving Yehoshua a double portion of his spirit, so Elisha makes his request.

Eliyahu says, "You have asked a very difficult thing. But this I promise you: if you still see me, if a vision of me still remains with you after I am taken from you, you will have a double portion of my spirit. And if not, not." Elisha sees a chariot of fire and horses of fire taking Eliyahu to heaven, and cries, "My father, my father, chariot and horsemen of Israel." He takes hold of his clothes and he tears them in two.

Rabbi Jonathan Sacks, chief rabbi of England, at a talk delivered in September of 1994, explained that based on the words of the Midrash, we understand the concept of immortality. The Midrash says, "Eliyahu did not really die." He continued to appear to the sages as a kind of living bond between earth and heaven. Why? Because his disciples kept his teachings alive. "If my vision stays with you even after I am gone, I will still be alive in your heart. If what I was, if what I did continues to inspire you, then you will still have a double portion of my spirit." This, Rabbi Sacks said, is in Jewish terms, immortality. I would simply add that this lesson isn't just for people like Elisha, who was a *tzaddik*. Each and every one of us has the capacity to be inspired with the vision of Torah, and to live life with the inspiration of Torah, achieving immortality and perfection.

6

Ego and Humility

Traditional Judaism and Chasidism have a very different approach to these two issues. I dare say that this difference is one of the main reasons why, over the last 250 years, many Traditional Jews have begun practicing a *chasidic* life-style.

However, before we delve into the result, let us discuss the issues from a traditional perspective. The Torah states that Moshe was the most humble person on the face of the earth. His humility was so great that it was the reason God chose him to be the leader of the Jewish people.

As the Midrash says, when Moshe was a shepherd, his devotion and dedication to his sheep foreshadowed his future concern for the Jewish people. It once happened that one of the sheep ran away. Moshe chased it for a long distance and finally caught up to it. At that very moment, God appeared to him from the burning bush and spoke to him. God's request was that he assume leadership and take the Jews out of Egypt. Why did God appear to him at the exact moment he finally caught the lost sheep?

MOSHE RABBEINU CHASING THE LOST SHEEP

The Lubavitcher Rebbe once explained that God saw Moshe's concern for a little lost sheep, that Moshe left everything else and didn't sleep or eat until he finally found it. This was the devotion that God was looking for in taking care of his chosen people. Only after this act of commitment and humility did God appear to him. All of Moshe's greatness, his knowledge, his compassion, didn't convince God that he was the right person for the job. It was his selfless dedication, which stemmed from a deep inner realization that God is everything, and Moshe was just a servant of God, that fitted him for the job.

Moshe's humility was his most important quality, and that was what made him the Jewish leader. When the Jews complained about not having food, Moshe answered them, *v'nachnu mah*—literally meaning "and what are we" that you complain to us. Chasidus explains these words to mean, "we are nothing."

Moshe, in asking, "Why are you complaining to us, after all who are we and what are we?" was sincerely expressing his view of himself. This sincere humility was what made Moshe able to lead the people and supply their needs, including food. His humility made it possible for the manna to come from heaven.

MOSHE RABBEINU: THE ULTIMATE EXPRESSION OF *BITTUL*, SELF-ABNEGATION

In regard to the complaint of the Jewish people that they had no meat in the desert, we find a similar explanation. The Torah (Numbers 11:13) quotes Moshe as saying, "From where do I have meat?" with the simple *(pshat)* meaning that "I can't give it to you because I don't have it myself." The Alter Rebbe explains that Moshe was also saying to the Jews that *meAyin,* from nothingness, you will get your meat. In other words, "It is the state of *ayin,* being nothing (humble), that will be the very cause of receiving the meat." It is only possible to receive God's blessing through humility.

Another example comes from Psalms 121:1. King Dovid asks, *"meAyin yovo ezri?"*—from where does my salvation come? Literally, King Dovid is asking God to help him, and he asks, "From where comes my help? My help comes from God." Chasidus, again, adds a deeper insight. What King Dovid was referring to was this state of *ayin,* which is the obliteration of the ego to the point that all that's left of one's personality is the level known as *ayin,* a complete subordination to the Divine. Clearly, King Dovid was *ayin* and did indeed receive God's help, as recorded in the Book of Psalms. And so he says himself: *meAyin*—through the state of self-nullification, *yovo ezri,* my salvation will come. He is not asking a question, he is telling us the solution to the problem.

MUST A JEWISH SCHOLAR HAVE SOME *GAIVA,* PRIDE?

The traditional view of pride considers it to be abhorrent. The talmudic sayings "He [the haughty person] and I [God] cannot live in the same home" (*Erechin* 15b) and "Possessing arrogance is tantamount to idol worship," make ego and arrogance unacceptable. However, there is a statement in Tractate *Sotah* (5a) that a *talmid chocham,* a learned Torah scholar, must have one-eighth of one-eighth measure of ego!

What does this mean? We just concluded that pride is out of the question! Also, why does the Talmud say that a *talmid chocham must* have some ego? I would think that if he wants to have some, fine, and if he doesn't want even an iota, that's even better.

The explanation to this puzzling statement is that the measure of ego that's prescribed is for the *talmid chocham* specifically. Since he is the one who has rid himself of any negative pride and ego, therefore it is only to such a person that the Talmud says, yes, you are the one who needs to stand up and make the point on behalf of Torah and God. In other words, there are two types of people with two types of ego, one being positive and the other negative.

GOOD STUDENTS SHOULD BE CAMP COUNSELORS

Here's a simple example: In our *yeshivah* we studied Torah throughout the year. We spent many long hours dissecting a couple of lines of the Talmud, and many late nights studying Chasidus. Around Shavuos (the festival celebrating the giving of the Torah), there was always a debate among our group of friends as to what we should do during the summer. Some contended that we should be counselors or travel to visit Jewish people in remote communities. Others argued that the place of a *yeshivah* student is in the *yeshivah,* not in a camp or anywhere else.

One of the good students approached his *mashpia,* spiritual counselor, who told him to go away from the *yeshivah* for the summer and be a counselor in a camp. He explained that it's important that a good student who loves learning, and would like to stay in the *yeshivah* for the summer to continue studying, be the one giving guidance to younger students and campers. The student who doesn't enjoy learning and doesn't know much Talmud and Chasidus is the one who needs to stay and learn during the summer months so that he can make up for all the information he didn't receive during the year.

This story gives some color to the idea that a *talmid chocham* must have some ego. He has to realize that he is the one who can and must impart the proper values and instruction to the Jewish people. At the same time, he realizes that from his personal point of view this is a difficult thing, because he would rather continue to commune with God and his Torah. His very lack of a "drive to power" draws people to him and makes them hear his words.

The true *talmid chocham* would rather not use any ego, however God says to him that he needs to use the ego, something that is an essential part of a human being, in a healthy and Jewish way. God wants pure ego, true ego, that can only come from a *talmid chocham*. Again, as in the example, only the committed, learned *yeshivah* student can communicate Torah properly. Therefore, it is he who should be a counselor, not the student who would rather be at camp anyway.

FIRST BE A *TALMID CHOCHAM* AND THEN BE CONCERNED WITH HAVING *GAIVA*

This concept of having some degree of pride is a good example of the difference in approach between

Traditional Judaism and Chasidism. Someone wrote a letter to Rabbi Yosef Yitzchok Schneerson saying that people in his shul made fun of him. He knew that he was someone who deserved respect, as required by Torah. Therefore, simply by being in shul, he was violating the prohibition "Don't put a stumbling block before the blind." What should he do?

The Rebbe responded that in regard to a *talmid chocham* having a degree of ego, there are two choices. Either one can become a *talmid chocham* and then incorporate some ego. Or, on the other hand, he can first make sure that he has the required modicum of ego, and, only after that, become a *talmid chocham*. The Rebbe concluded the letter by suggesting the first approach.

The Rebbe was showing this person that it is petty to approach the idea of the requisite "Torah Ego" from a selfish point of view. Therefore, the Rebbe told him to first begin by being a true *talmid chocham* and then be concerned about the required amount of ego.

This attitude has the ultimate result of making true selflessness possible. When such a person is called upon by God to stand up and say something the way it needs to be said, he not only has no difficulty, but does it with energy and joy. He has, not ego, but the true strength and self-confidence of the Torah.

THE TRADITIONAL RESPONSE TO THE TALMUD'S REQUIREMENT OF HAVING *GAIVA*

When a Traditional Jew reads this story and its explanation, he can ask a simple yet strong question. If the Talmud says a *talmid chocham* has to have some ego, then why should this individual not be concerned about the situation in his shul? After all, his Torah rights are being abused. Also, is he not at least partially guilty of *lifnei iver,* do not put a stumbling block before a person? This is exactly the point. From a traditional perspective, one must make the emphasis that his ego should not be stepped on. On the other hand, from a chasidic vantage point, let me not be so concerned about whether or not my ego is being put down. Let me not be concerned that people don't have what we call *Kovod haTorah,* respect for the Torah that's within me.

CHASIDIM DO NOT MAKE A BIG DEAL ABOUT HAVING ACCEPTABLE GAIVA

The reason *chasidim* consider this an unimportant issue, is that people are too close to themselves to say objectively that it is their "required ego" that is being abused. The fact is that we are frail human beings and when someone upsets us, or says something that is contrary to our way of thinking, it is presumably not the *Kovod haTorah* that bothers us, but something much simpler, the (negative) human ego and pride. Therefore, the Rebbe suggests that we concentrate on the positive energy within Torah. We are too subjective to separate the two types of ego, particularly when we are feeling hurt or embarrassed.

KOVOD HATORAH FROM A CHASIDIC PERSPECTIVE

Chasidim go a step further. The feeling is that looking to protect one's so-called *Kovod haTorah* is simply repugnant. This is "between the lines." The word *repugnant* is a harsh word, but when one understands the importance of being humble, the repugnance of ego can be appreciated. This is why in *chasidic* circles the concept of *Kovod haTorah* has not developed any great importance as a guide to daily human relations.

REMOVAL OF PRIDE AND CONCEIT

This leads us to another basic development, in which Chasidus goes beyond *Mussar,* ethical teachings. In books of *Mussar,* there is the concept of *bittul haGaiva,* the removal of pride and conceit. This idea, explains the previous Lubavitcher Rebbe (in his letters vol. 4, pp. 524–536), is an *avodah gufnis,* an act that involves the body. *Mussar* gives practical instructions, which, if implemented truthfully, will help get rid of coarse, unrefined pride.

These coarse forms of pride include the boastful feelings that *b'nei Torah,* learned Torah scholars, can have about their knowledge, and the assumption of the wealthy that they deserve respect, since, after all, they were blessed with wealth. In addition, there are people who have no knowledge, and no money either, yet they walk around believing in themselves. They have convinced themselves, and believe they are fooling others, that they are important people. All of these symptoms of conceit necessitate what *Mussar* calls *bittul haGaiva,* the complete removal of these arrogant feelings.

YESHUS, A REFINED FORM OF *GAIVA*

Then there are three expressions of what Chasidus calls *yeshus,* literally egohood, a more refined form of *gaiva,* arrogance. Deep down, the people who possess these forms of *yeshus* are disappointed that no one notices how great they are.

The first type doesn't even talk about himself or his virtues. His character is too refined for that. The second will go out of his way to conceal his good qualities. He understands the importance of humility. The third not only hides his greatness but also does things to make people think he is very ordinary or even coarse. He mixes with people and sincerely tries to learn from everyone, even those who may know much less than he.

From the point of view of *Mussar,* these are superior people. However, Chasidus considers them to be suffering from spiritual sickness, in that their image in the eyes of others (and themselves) still matters to them. True, they have good qualities, especially the third, but this very fact makes the diagnosis and cure of their ailment more difficult. What's necessary here is an *avodah ruchnis,* a spiritual, not just a bodily act, to eliminate this hidden *gaiva.* The focus of their attention must be taken off the self, by self-nullification to something higher.

BITTUL MEANS (A) SURRENDER AND (B) DEDICATION

This *avodah* is known as *bittul haYesh,* the surrender of the self. The Rebbe goes a step further, emphasizing that the word *bittul* has two meanings, surrender and dedication. The first step is to get rid of his refined arrogance. Only after that's been accomplished can one proceed to take the *yesh,* the self, and dedicate it to God through Torah and *mitzvos.* This is done through the dedication of the mind and heart to the service of God. By committing the mind and heart to God, one incorporates the "self" in the service of God. Therefore, the proper translation of *bittul ha Yesh* is the surrender of the self.

This translation is correct because, according to Chasidus, the self, *yesh,* must be incorporated in the service of God, not eliminated. "Surrender" means to give one's self away, not to destroy it. That is the *avodah* known as *bittul ha Yesh.* Only after this *avodah* can one proceed to unite his ego with God. However, prior to the *avodah* of dedicating the mind and heart to a higher purpose, namely, God, one must completely get rid of the subtle arrogance, which is a form of selfishness. This prerequisite is also called *bittul,* but in the sense of surrender.

In summary, Traditional Judaism deals with the removal of simple arrogance; in the previous Rebbe's terminology, this is a service of the body, a set of procedures. *Mussar* gives the proper advice to successfully accomplish this task. But to remove the subtle ego, and to take the "self" itself and dedicate it to God, necessitates the study of Chasidus.

7

Reward and Punishment

In order to understand the perspectives of Traditional and chasidic Judaism on the issue of reward and punishment, it is necessary to elaborate on some of the differences between the teachings of *Mussar* and Chasidus. It is Mussar, by and large, that has shaped the view of Traditional Judaism in regard to reward and punishment; let us understand what *Mussar* is and says.

MUSSAR, CHASTISEMENT

Mussar teaches a person to reject and negate the physical. It is predicated on the subjugation of the material by demonstrating its unworthy grossness. This includes any improper propensities such as overindulgence in food and drink and other physical delights. Man shares these desires with animals, but when he acts like them he sinks below their level. Animals lack the rationality

71

that is required to desire anything more than the gratification of the body, but man is endowed with the intelligence to aspire to something higher, to intellectual values and moral virtues. Thus, when he prefers physical pleasures, he is lower than the animal.

This school of thought, which rejects the material by depicting the baseness of physical pleasures and passions, and by describing their dire consequences, is the school of *Mussar*.

Some of the Rabbis who taught and established the modern day *Mussar* movement include Rabbi Yisrael Lipkin of Salant (1809–1883), Rabbi Zisel of Kelm, known as the Alter of Kelm (1824–1898), Rabbi Yosef Hurwitz of Novardok, known as the Alter of Novardok (1848–1920), Rabbi Nosson Finkel of Slobodka, known as the Alter of Slobodka (1849–1927), Rabbi Eliyahu Lapian (1876–1970), and Rabbi Eliyahu Dessler (1892–1953).

FIRE AND BRIMSTONE

Another fundamental approach that is found in early *Mussar* writings such as *Shaarei Teshuvah* by Rabbeinu Yona of Gerona, Spain (1180–1263), *Chovos Halevavos* by Rabbi Bachyah Ibn Pakudah of Spain (early 11th century), and *Raishis Chochmah* by Rabbi Eliyahu de Vidas of Amsterdam (1708), is the emphasis on severe punishments for sins. *Mussar* doesn't mince any words; it is very direct in letting the person know what he will need to experience prior to entering *Gan Eden,* Paradise, after "one hundred and twenty years" (or more, we hope!). *Mussar* discusses at length the kind of punishments the soul will get for sinning. It talks about the "fire" that will burn the person for his iniquities, and brings to the forefront the negative consequences that take place when one commits a sin. To oversimplify slightly, *Mussar* scares the person; it holds that emphasizing the fire and brimstone will get people to commit fewer and less severe sins. For some examples, see *Raishis Chochmah, Shaar ha'kedusha,* Chapter 17, and *Shaar ha'anova,* Chapter 2, as well as *Chovos Halivovos, Shaar Haprishus*—gate of self-denial.

Of course, reward and punishment is a basic principle of the Torah. However, one can place the emphasis on the body and its shortcomings, or one can focus on the soul and its infinite potential for influencing the body. The approach of *Mussar* tends to dwell on emphasizing the body's coarsening and weakening impact on the soul.

The Baal Shem Tov gave the following analogy for the difference between Chasidus and *Mussar.* When a thief comes to steal there are two approaches. One is for the owner to begin shouting. The thief becomes afraid and runs away, but it is quite possible that he will return and try again. The second approach is for the owner to capture the thief and turn him into an honest person. This second approach is the accomplishment of Chasidus. The thief does not return, since he is no longer a thief.

CHASIDUS: THE REVELATION OF THE *NESHOMAH*

Chasidus emphasizes the positive. It concentrates on the soul. It explains how one can achieve the greatest union with God, which will automatically overcome the difficulties caused by the corporeal body. It accomplishes this inwardly, by teaching concepts that go beyond conventional wisdom, even that of the Torah, as interpreted from within a traditional perspective.

Chasidus enlightens us with explanations of such ideas as God's unity, the purpose of creation, how we got here, why we are here, and many more questions which force us to confront the unknown. However deep and unfathomable they are, these issues have tremendous impact on us in our day-to-day lives, and it is therefore everyone's responsibility to learn as much as they can about what the Torah says about them, just as everyone needs to know which foods are kosher. In fact, we only eat three times a day, but the *mitzvos* connected with these concepts are constant *(Sefer HaChinuch)*.

Chasidus supplies answers, or at least gives one the tools to deal with these issues, awakening the *neshomah,* so that it is quite possible for one to wake up one morning and reject the base, animalistic desires. How did it happen? After all, the person didn't focus on how bad they are!

Chasidus says that concentrating on the negativity in life is itself negative and will never truly succeed in eliminating one's animal drive. The paradox is that one gets too involved with negativity to get rid of it. It is similar to someone who is engaged in an argument with an unethical person who feels free to use sophistry, lies, and character assassination. The more the good person involves himself in the other's words, the more he stands to lose. Some of the dirt and filth is bound to rub off and stick to him!

Chasidus teaches that if one spends time on one's base desires and lusts and does not achieve a decisive victory, he has lost more than he has gained. However, putting energy into the positive produces immediate gains and ultimate success. By studying the *neshomah,* its creativity, its greatness, its potential excellence, the entire focus of one's attention has shifted. He has moved into a world that promotes goodness and holiness, a world characterized by light.

THE SPIRIT OF THE HUMAN AND THE ANIMAL

This difference in approach between *Mussar* and Chasidus is supported by a verse in *Koheles* (Ecclesiastes 3:21) written by King Shlomo. He says, "The spirit of man ascends upward and the spirit of the animal descends downward." This simply means that the human spirit wants to be close to God and the spirit of the animal desires closeness to earthiness. In our context this can be explained in the following way: The spirit of man rising upward, meaning the natural desire that the *neshomah* has, always desires attachment to something higher than itself. The *neshomah* is eager to be absorbed in the unknown, it doesn't mind being consumed by a greater revelation, namely that of God.

On the other hand, the spirit of the animal, who is constantly looking downward, refers to the animal drive within the Jew that desires more and more material pleasures. This search motivates an intellectual inquiry into the material world as it exists. Chasidus teaches that the animal drive isn't interested in how the matter got here, or why it's here. Its only interest is, that indeed, it *is* here, and therefore I can enjoy it, period. This is the meaning of "the spirit of the animal descends downward," it constantly looks to what is known and observable rather than looking to the unknown and abstract.

REB YISRAEL SALANTER, THE FOUNDER OF THE *MUSSAR* MOVEMENT

To better understand *Mussar*'s approach to reward and punishment, let us introduce a teaching of Rabbi Yisrael Lipkin of Salant, also known as Reb Yisrael Salanter, the founder of the modern-day *Mussar* movement. Reb Yisrael, himself an accomplished talmudist and dean of a *yeshivah,* was a descendant of the Vilna Gaon. Reb Yisrael's writings are compiled in his book, *Or Yisrael.* Rabbi Avraham Yaakov Finkel, in his book, *The Great Torah Commentators,* quotes the following selection from Reb Yisrael's commentary on *Bereishis* 5:24. The Torah states: "Chanoch walked with God, and he was no more, because God had taken him."

Reb Yisrael comments:

Chanoch walked with God; our rabbis in Midrash *Talpiot* tell us, "Chanoch was a shoemaker, and with every single stitch that he made he achieved mystical unions with his creator." This Midrash cannot possibly mean that while he was sitting and stitching shoes for his customers, he was concentrating on mystical concepts. This would be forbidden by Torah law. How could he divert his attention to other matters while engaged in work he had been hired to do by others? No, the mystical unions were actually the attention he devoted to each and every stitch, making sure that it would be good and strong and that the pair of shoes he was making would be a good pair, giving comfort and pleasure to whoever would wear it.

Rabbi Finkel adds the following comment: ". . . This interpretation is typical of Rabbi Yisrael Salanter's approach. Man achieves 'mystical union' and attaches himself to God by emulating God's attributes, lavishing goodness and kindness on others, treating them with honesty and fairness." I'd like to add several points to enhance the understanding of the Midrash *Talpiot,* so that we can clearly see the chasidic approach to the Midrash, and realize that the difference between the founder of the *Mussar* movement's view and the chasidic view, depends on their basic approach to character development, as explained earlier.

WHAT ARE *KAVANOS?*

The Kabbalah says that each and every *mitzvah* performed in this physical world causes *yichudim,* unions in the spiritual realms. These *yichudim* are unifications of God's name and energy with the physical object involved. The direct cause of the *yichudim* are the *kavanos,* the spiritual intentions prior to and during the actual deed. For example, before certain *mitzvos,* such as the counting of the *Omer,* and at the beginning of *davening,* it is the custom of many Jews to say, "for the purpose of the unification of God's sacred name, *Yud Hay* with *Vav Hay* . . ."

Chasidus does not emphasize the details of *kavanos* and *yichudim,* since they are not for everyone. For example, the *siddur* used by Chabad Lubavitcher *chasidim* is based on Rabbi Shneur Zalman's extensive research of sixty other *siddurim,* most of them kabbalistically oriented. However, Reb Shneur Zalman, in his Siddur, didn't openly include the kabbalistic *kavanos* and *yichudim,* implying that the ordinary person is not obligated to say or think those *kavanos.* Rather, by reading the simple text and knowing the meaning of the words, he receives the spiritual benefit just as if he were reciting the actual *kavanos* and *yichudim.* Unless a person has permission from his teachers to learn the actual *kavanos,* he is encouraged to rely on the general intention of asking God to accept his prayer as if he had performed all the *kavanos.*

KAVANOS ARE NECESSARY FOR ALL PHYSICAL ACTS

Based on this, let us understand the Midrash. Chanoch, who was a *tzaddik,* was given a pair of shoes to repair. Knowing quite well the appropriate *kavanos* needed to elevate these shoes, he went ahead and used his own discretion and had the spiritual *kavanos* in order to properly accomplish not just the repair of the shoes, but more importantly, the spiritual repair that the one who wore these shoes needed. Chanoch knew that the person who gave him the shoes was delighted that he would perform the *kavanos.* He could have gone to an ordinary shoemaker, but he came to Chanoch because he desired a total transformation of character so that he could feel spiritually well enough to walk around in those shoes.

Therefore he came to Chanoch, who was a *tzaddik,* and didn't go to the shoemaker on the corner. From his perspective, if Chanoch wouldn't have had the *kavanos,* then he would have felt cheated, since his primary reason was spiritual not physical. So to answer the question of how Chanoch was allowed to take time away from the job to meditate on the *kavanos,* it was not stealing, God forbid. The truth of the matter is, for a customer of Chanoch, repairing shoes without *kavanos* was equivalent to not doing the job properly. Since the person chose Chanoch as his shoemaker, his intention was clear, "I need a spiritual repair and if that's done I'll have a good pair of shoes."

MUSSAR: DON'T MIX *KAVANOS* WITH WORK

What still remains unresolved is where Reb Yisrael Salanter is coming from. Reb Yisrael was a great Torah scholar and a descendent of the Vilna Gaon. The Gaon was steeped in Kabbalah to the extent that he writes (see *Even Shlomo* 8:21 and the Vilna Gaon's commentary on *Mishlei* 5:18) that anyone who doesn't study the esoteric wisdom (Kabbalah) can have no clarity in the exoteric, simple understanding of Torah. But if he is not clear in his understanding, how could he give a halachic ruling?!

Since Reb Yisrael was aware of the Vilna Gaon's clear instruction, and allowed himself to give halachic rulings, surely he was knowledgeable in Kabbalah. So the question remains, how does Reb Yisrael derive his interpretation of the Midrash *Talpiot?*

At first glance it seems that he doesn't take into consideration the importance of *kavanos.* This is implied by the fact that he says that Chanoch's *kavanos* weren't spiritual in nature, but rather very down-to-earth. Chanoch's *kavanos* involved thinking about making a better pair of shoes in the literal sense! Rabbi Finkel suggested that Reb Yisrael's response follows his overall view in regard to ethics and character development, emulating God by being honest and kind. This also explains that Reb Yisrael feels the way he does not just in this case, but in many other cases as well.

Nevertheless, why does he seemingly brush off the importance of spiritual *kavanos* for the purpose of emulating God? Aren't *kavanos* important from God's perspective?

It seems to me that Reb Yisrael is saying that *kavanos* are important and essential. However, there is a time and place for them. He feels that they are inappropriate during work hours. What he means is that one cannot mix spirituality and physicality, because from a *Mussar* perspective one needs to put the emphasis on the ethics in a direct manner. Chanoch, given shoes to repair, had his first obligation to be honest and only think about the shoes, so that the stitches would be stronger and better in the literal sense. Mussar sees the mixing of *ruchnius,* spirituality, and *gashmius,* physicality, as a contradiction. Let *ruchnius* be *ruchnius* and *gashmius* be *gashmius.* Therefore, Reb Yisrael, who was aware of the Kabbalah and respected the holiness and importance of *kavanos,* felt that in the case of Chanoch, it was inappropriate to mix the two worlds.

CHASIDUS: *RUCHNIUS* AND *GASMIUS* ARE ONE

Chasidus has a very different approach to *ruchnius* and *gashmius.* Chasidus emphasizes the value of purified matter (physical matter that is dedicated to a higher, spiritual purpose, and thus ceases to be merely physical), and of form when embodied in matter (the spiritual that influences and elevates physical matter, and itself is no longer merely ethereal). In this union of matter and form there is no beginning or end, superior or inferior; each is essential to the other, each is implanted within the other. One God created them both for the identical purpose of revealing His holy light, and only in perfect unity do they achieve the perfection He desired. The aim of Chasidus is the perception of the essential qualities of form and substance. It leads to the dominance of form over substance to the extent that substance itself becomes form, physical matter becomes a vehicle for godliness.

This idea is expressed in the famous interpretation of the Baal Shem Tov on the verse in the book of *Shemos,* "If you shall see your enemy's donkey carrying a load, you shall help him [unload it]." The Baal Shem explained that the enemy refers to the animal drive within the Jew, who is always finding ways to get him to go against God's ways. Don't just say, "I'll have nothing to do with it, I'll mind my business and allow it to get hurt." Rather, "You shall help him," meaning, get involved and redirect the animal drive's desires from negative to positive. Harness it, work with it, elevate it, but just don't say, "Let it be bad, and I'll be good."

This is a basic premise in Chasidism. A person needs to incorporate the physical and the spiritual, the *ruchnius* and the *gashmius.* Otherwise, the body is going in one direction and the *neshomah* is going in another. Chasidus teaches that this approach to God isn't just for the synagogue and the *yeshivah,* rather it's for all times and all places. That's why Chasidus demands a mixing of work and *kavanos,* because it is the ultimate purpose.

ONLY YOUR HANDS, NOT YOUR MIND

When Chasidus encourages the involvement of the animal drive in serving God, this would seem to imply that one's entire being should be occupied with one's work. After all, if one really wants to assist the donkey who is lost and astray, one needs to go all out and get involved with one's mind and heart. However, Chasidus quotes the verse in Psalms 128:2, "the toil of your *hands* will enable you to eat," to mean limiting one's involvement in physical matters, to the use of the hands only, meaning a person shouldn't be concerned and anxious about their work to the extent that it is the constant background of his or her life. This total involvement is reserved for one's service of God. Hands here refers to the effort and energy needed for the job, be it plowing a field, programming a computer, or arguing a case in court.

It's understood that in order to do a good job, one needs to concentrate and focus the mind, but on the other hand, the amount of mind needed for the hands to be successful is limited. When one puts all of his infinite spiritual potential into worldly goals, which by nature are finite, he is definitely trying too hard, and cannot expect true success. One can do an excellent job by using that part of the mind which is a guide and tool in directing and harnessing the hands.

From a Torah perspective, someone who is "working for a living," and whose work requires great involvement, needs to know that the ultimate objective isn't the work, but rather Torah and the service of God. The intent that God had in wanting us to work for a living isn't the work itself.

Chasidus teaches that the person who is working and keeps this attitude has a greater revelation of God than even the Torah scholar! In addition to the reason advanced by Traditional Judaism, that he can support the Torah scholars and share credit for their achievement, he or she has other advantages. The discipline and skills learned at work will ultimately transfer to the realms of holiness. Placed in the world, he constantly sees God's divine providence, how everything is directed by Him. Being involved with *yishuv haolom,* the civilizing of the world, there is an opportunity to influence those he meets in the course of the day, whether by being a living example or actively sharing Torah and its *mitzvos.*

Quantitatively speaking, to work with the hands means to take any gift of free time to learn and do *mitzvos* rather than look for more work to do, and in the qualitative sense, making the high point of the day those few hours or minutes in which one does have a chance to learn. If the ultimate pleasure is climbing the ladder and getting a promotion, a person is operating with a very restricted idea of pleasure.

Therefore, at the very same time that Chasidus believes in the combination of work and *kavanah,* one must not forget which is primary. The ultimate objective is to emulate Chanoch. He repaired the shoes, in the literal sense, yet the motivation and inspiration was the *kavanos.* So, too, every person can go out into the world and use the material and physical as a tool for implementing God's will.

REB LEVI YITZCHOK OF BERDITCHEV: OUR "DEFENSE ATTORNEY"

To return to the attitude of always emphasizing the positive, the *neshomah,* there is a story about the great *tzaddik,* Rabbi Levi Yitzchok of Berditchev, which crystallizes this. Once Reb Levi Yitzchok was walking in the street. He noticed a Jew *davening*. What was unusual about this particular Jew's *davening* was that at the very same time he was sitting on the ground and applying a thick coat of grease to the rear axle of his wagon. Reb Levi Yitzchok, realizing this, shouted out, as though he were speaking to someone standing in front of him, "God, look at your beautiful Jews, even in the middle of their work they praise you through *davening!*"

Now one might wonder, what's so great about Reb Levi Yitzchok's approach, after all, didn't he say an untruth? The answer is most definitely no! From his perspective, a Jew is perfect and one should always look at another Jew with the "right" eye, always attempting to find the good. He saw this Jew's true soul and told the truth as he saw it.

He was also teaching us that whatever a Jew does that involves his relationship with God, it is between himself and God. It is not someone else's business to be judgmental and ask him how he dares to fix his wheels in middle of *davening*. It might be a true assessment, but only a close, intimate friend has any business in pointing out how what he is doing is not worthy of him. One is to only find the good, the *neshomah* that is pure and holy. This is the chasidic attitude towards another Jew.

LOVE YOUR FRIEND AS YOURSELF

To better understand where Rabbi Levi Yitzchok was coming from when he seemingly reversed the truth, it is necessary to introduce a teaching of Rabbi Shneur Zalman in the *Tanya,* Chapter 32. He says that when the

Torah says, "rebuke, shall you rebuke your friend," this doesn't refer to someone who considers himself to be a friend only in worldly matters. Specifically, it means a friend in issues dealing with the learning of Torah and the doing of *mitzvos*. The Alter Rebbe derives this from the Hebrew word used in this verse, *Amitecho,* which contains two words, *im (she)'itecho,* "people" (that) "are with you," meaning that they are together in all issues, from the physical to the spiritual.

Only such a friend should be rebuked, otherwise the rebuke is not to a friend, but to a stranger! One might think he is acting as a friend, but unless a relationship has been developed in all areas of life, one has no business rebuking. This was at the heart of Reb Levi Yitzchok's philosophy. He didn't know this person, and as far as he was concerned, this Jew didn't know any better. What he could do and should do, was to say something positive, because the truth of the matter, as revealed in Chasidus, is that a Jew is only good.

Mussar, on the other hand, is forced to take note of the negative, and furthermore has a tendency to make it into a major issue. Possibly that is why Reb Yisrael Salanter questioned Chanoch's behavior. Through extreme thoroughness in obviating any possible negative consequences, the conclusion could be reached that having spiritual *kavanos* during work is improper.

PUNISHMENT FROM A *MUSSAR* PERSPECTIVE

The difference in attitude towards reward and punishment between Chasidus and *Mussar* is one of emphasis. Fundamental to both is the Torah, which clearly states that one will be rewarded for *mitzvos* and punished for sins. The Torah enumerates in great detail the various punishments, as well as the rewards.

Mussar feels the emphasis should be placed on the punishment for sin. Just as *Mussar* highlights the spiritual by contrasting it with the baseness of the material, it motivates good conduct by looking at the consequences of bad conduct.

Chasidus, on the other hand, brings out the inherent value of the spiritual and the good. It compares, contrasts, and explains all sorts of good and holy things. For instance, a chasidic discourse may devote itself to understanding how the "good man" differs from the "kind man" or the "giving man," and to the sources of these personalities in God's holy *sefirot*. By understanding differences between the good, the better, and the best, the student of Chasidus becomes accustomed to living in a world of light, of positive, life-affirming values.

Chasidus shows how goodness and holiness can be found in every Jew, without exception. *Tanya,* Chapter 11, teaches us that even someone who is completely evil still possesses a divine soul which hovers over him, even though it cannot express itself through his body until he does *teshuvah,* the return from wrongdoing.

The author is clearly alluding to the fact that it's never too late for anyone to return to God. In fact, he quotes the Talmud, that whenever ten Jewish people get together, regardless of their purpose in gathering and regardless of their moral level from a halachic perspective, yet the *Shechinah,* the Divine Presence, dwells among them! This principle underlies human relations between the Jewish people. As the Rambam says in the laws of *Sanhedrin* (25:2), "Though they may be common and lowly, they are children of Abraham, Isaac, and Jacob, and 'The Hosts of God' whom he took out of Egypt with great strength and a strong arm."

PUNISHMENT FROM A CHASIDIC PERSPECTIVE

As far as punishment is concerned, from a chasidic view it can be called a "spiritual washing machine." In some chasidic circles it is known as *tikunim,* meaning corrective practices for the purpose of a total cleansing of the *neshomah.* Prior to entering *Gan Eden,* Paradise, the soul needs to get rid of all the stains it received during its life on earth. It's inappropriate to go to a special meeting with the king while dressed in dirty clothing. In the same vein, when one is about to enter the inner chamber of God's abode, which is Paradise, it is inappropriate to come covered with spiritual dirt. Therefore, the *neshomah* goes through a "washing machine" which may contain hot water, cold water, solvents, surfactants and abrasives, plus a lot of agitation, so that it can enter Paradise and join the "company." Chasidus spends little time on the details of the various punishments, because this is not the emphasis. The main thing is the potential for everyone to reveal the *neshomah,* which is pure goodness.

PRACTICAL REWARD FROM A *MUSSAR* PERSPECTIVE

In regard to the reward for doing *mitzvos,* in most *yeshivos* which follow the Lithuanian, *Mussar* approach to Talmud study, as laid down by the Vilna Gaon and his students, the students are encouraged by their teachers and deans to study diligently so that they may end up being a Vilna Gaon or a Rabbi Akiva Eiger!

This approach has been recorded by Professor Samuel Heilman of Queens College, a social anthropologist. In his book, *Defenders of the Faith* (Schocken, 1992, p. 263), he asked a nonchasidic *rosh yeshivah,* the dean of the school, "What are the goals of the *yeshivah* and its education?" The *rosh yeshivah* responded, "Our way is not a goal-oriented education. We learn Torah, period." Professor Heilman asked him, "But not everyone can become a scholar?" He responded, "But that is the goal." He smiled and pointed to the wall behind Heilman, at a picture of the founder of the *yeshivah.* "He used to say that the *mitzvah* of learning Torah is not that you should learn or even that you should set specific times to review Torah. The *mitzvah* is that everybody should become a *Gaon,* master of the texts, if he has the power to be one. Nobody knows if he is capable of becoming one. So on one hand it is not goal-oriented education; in another respect it's the most powerfully motivated education possible. . . . Everyone is duty bound to become the greatest possible *talmid chocham.*"

This remarkable approach has motivated thousands of students to delve into the "ocean of the Talmud." They are told that the reward for spending another hour learning a page of Talmud, rather than playing basketball, is the possibility of becoming another Vilna Gaon! Another *Gadol,* great Torah sage!

This attitude has its drawbacks as well. When one does not succeed in becoming a great sage or scholar, and instead becomes a business person, the feeling is that he "has not made it," and that one should have pity and compassion for such a person. Although he is also encouraged to use his business acumen in the support of Torah learning, this is clearly a secondary position.

The attitude of the *Bnei Torah* (a term referring to those who sit and learn Torah as their occupation and do not involve themselves in the mundane, physical world) towards the ones who have not made it in the learning world leaves much to be desired!

REWARD FROM A CHASIDIC PERSPECTIVE

In chasidic *yeshivos,* the attitude is totally opposite. Certainly, one needs to learn Talmud day and night, however, not because there is some reward awaiting him, or that he will become a great genius of Talmud, who will eventually come up with creative insights and novelties that even Moshe Rabbeinu was never aware of! For *chasidim,* the story of Reb Zusia of Annipol is the example to live by. Reb Zusia would always say, ''I am not concerned that after my lifetime, when I come before the heavenly court, they will ask me why I wasn't like Avrohom, Yitzchok, Yaccov, etc. Rather, I am concerned that they will ask me, 'Why weren't you, Zusia, the way *you, Zusia,* could have been?'!''

This attitude emphasizes that every Jew, whether Torah learner or businessperson, is equally important in God's eyes, and therefore, the one who sits and learns Torah all day must look at the businessperson, not as a second-class citizen who has not made it in the Jewish world, but rather as a first-class citizen who is serving God in the same qualitative way. Therefore, no pity and compassion is necessary on the scholar's part. On the contrary, it could well be that the businessperson is more in touch with God than the scholar. The reason being, the businessperson sees God's providence and relies on His help daily in his contact with mundane realities. The scholar, however, sitting in a *yeshivah* with an assured income and a regular daily schedule, is sheltered from the opportunity to experience God so directly.

This attitude derives from two concepts: Divine Providence, *Hashgochah Protis,* and the making of a Home for God on Earth, *dirah bitachtonim.* These concepts are elaborated in Chapter 2 of this book and Chapter 7 of my other book, *Demystifying the Mystical* (Jason Aronson, 1995).

The same is true as far as the chasidic attitude toward *mitzvos.* The reason for observing the *mitzvos* isn't to become someone else, even if that someone else is as holy and knowledgeable as the Vilna Gaon or Rabbi Akiva Eiger. Rather, it is to achieve the oneness of God and man that is achieved by doing the *mitzvos.*

In chasidic literature the focus was, is, and will always be the relationship between the Jew and his God. By way of analogy, a child may desire a candy, but its real need is for a true relationship with its parents. There is a story of the fifth Lubavitcher Rebbe, Reb Sholom Ber, that will help illustrate this. When he was small, his grandfather, Reb Menachem Mendel, the Tzemach Tzedek, used to give him candies as a reward for learning well. The candies were *chometz,* barley sugar, and when it came Pesach time, his parents found that the little boy had saved all the candies, because to him they symbolized his closeness to his grandfather and his grandfather's happiness with him. They had to persuade him to eat them. This is the chasidic idea of reward. Even though the candies may be sweet, the closeness with God is sweeter.

In the same way, what a Jew really wants and needs is closeness with God. This, the Alter Rebbe explains in

Tanya, is the meaning of "The reward for a *mitzvah* is the *mitzvah* itself." The word *mitzvah* is related to *tzavta,* connection. The reward for doing a *mitzvah* is the connection which is made with God, a deeper dimension of attachment.

For example, when a person distributes *tzedakah,* his will is completely identified with God's will that this poor person be helped. Not only that, the hand that distributes *tzedakah,* since it is carrying out God's will, is at that moment completely united with God. It is as if God Himself were distributing the *tzedakah.* Similarly with all of the *mitzvos,* each unites various powers of the soul and body with God. When a Jew does a *mitzvah,* not only his soul, but his body is godly. The more his body expresses the truth of his soul, the more he is truly himself.

III

THE PRACTICAL

8

Moshiach

After discussing the philosophical differences between Traditional Judaism and Chasidism, it is appropriate to conclude with some practical examples of the way in which chasidic Judaism has developed, within the framework of Torah.

We will begin with the varying attitudes in the Jewish community toward the issue of *Moshiach*. The coming of *Moshiach* is a fundamental principle of the Torah. In fact, it is the fulfillment of the purpose of creation. The traditional view of *Moshiach* has its roots in the thirteen articles of Jewish faith, which the Rambam in his commentary on the Mishnah (*Sanhedrin,* Chapter 10) refers to as "the fundamental truths of our religion and its very foundation." Many Jews recite these thirteen articles daily. They are known as the *Ani Maamin's,* I Believe's. Article twelve is the belief in the arrival of the *Moshiach* and the *Moshiach* era.

ONE OF THE THIRTEEN ARTICLES OF FAITH

Yet, not withstanding the fact that there are thirteen articles, it is article twelve that has been propounded, discussed, and debated more than all the others. The exact text found in most prayer books is, *"Ani ma-amin bemuna sheleima b'bias hamoshiach, v'af al pe sheyismameah im kol ze achaka lo bcol yom shey-ovo,"* "I believe with complete faith in the coming of *Moshiach*. And although he may tarry, nevertheless I await daily for him to come." This is what the Jews sang in the "camps," not the immutability or eternity of God.

Why this emphasis throughout our history? Isn't it enough to believe in *Moshiach's* coming, or does one have to eagerly anticipate his arrival? The word in the article is "await"; what exactly does it mean?

RAMBAM'S VIEW OF
AWAITING *MOSHIACH'S* ARRIVAL

The Rambam, in his *Mishneh Torah* (Laws of Kings, Chapter 11), elucidates this, saying, "And all those who do not believe in the *Moshiach* or do not await his coming, not only do they deny the truth of the words of the prophets, but they reject the truth of the entire Torah and our teacher Moshe." The Rambam makes it crystal clear that believing in *Moshiach* without await-ing his arrival is tantamount to rejecting Torah!

The Rambam has been accepted by Traditional Ju-daism as the authority on the laws of *Moshiach*. Even though *halachah* normally says to follow the opinion of the author of the Code of Jewish law, known as the

Mechaber, the Compiler, Rabbi Yosef Caro, yet in matters where the *Mechaber* hasn't ruled, we follow the opinion of the authority who has done so. Therefore, in regard to all laws and details associated with *Moshiach,* we follow the Rambam, who is the sole authority.

GREAT JEWISH RABBIS' VIEWS ON AWAITING THE ARRIVAL OF *MOSHIACH*

Before we explore the chasidic view of *Moshiach,* I'd like to quote several traditional scholars on the topic of *Moshiach,* showing the unanimous acceptance of the need to do anything and everything possible to hasten the coming of *Moshiach.*

Chida'a the Sephardi

Rabbi Chaim Yosef Dovid Azulai—*Chida'a*—haSephardi writes in his *Midbar Kadamot,* in the section dealing with *kivu,* hope, "We all believe with complete faith that tomorrow morning the sun will shine and bring light. One can wonder, how do we know this? Does the sun's shining today necessitate its shining tomorrow? Yes, for it is so written in the Torah, 'day and night shall not cease.' Is there any greater faith than this? God Almighty declares, 'I swear that my glory will fill the entire world!' Our God guarantees that there will be a day that the glory of God will fill the entire universe. Surely we must believe this, for it will bring greater hope that perhaps today is the awaited day. We should believe in the establishment of God's Kingdom in the entire world with the same certainty with which we await the daily rising of the sun. It is upon us to await and anticipate that great day!"

The Brisk View

Rabbi Yitzchok Zeev M'Brisk is quoted in the *Bais Halevi Haggadah,* page 120:

It is written in the thirteen principles of faith of the Rambam, "I believe in the coming of *Moshiach* . . . and even though He may tarry, I wait for him every day." There are those that ask, "Why is this principle, of all the thirteen, written with an objection and an answer to that objection?" In truth, there is no objection. It is a description of the real meaning of faith in *Moshiach.* It is not enough to believe in the concept—it is necessary to look forward to His coming every day. As the Rambam writes in another place, "Whoever doesn't look forward to His coming is a heretic."

The Gaon Rav Yitzchok Zeev of Brisk used to constantly repeat that it's not enough to believe that He will come, but as is said three times a day in prayer, "We hope for Your salvation *all day.*" Yearning for *Moshiach* is literally every moment of every day!

Zohar

The *Zohar,* in *parshas Bereshis,* says, "A voice is heard from the heavens, 'Who amongst you awaits each day for the redemption?' And one that doesn't await *Moshiach* each day in this world will not merit the world to come!"

Chofetz Chaim, Author of
Mishnah B'erurah and *Shmiras Haloshon*

The Chofetz Chaim, in his explanations on the *siddur,* page 168, says: "It shouldn't suffice to request but instead, we should demand the redemption. . . . Several times a day we request in our prayers the redemption. Nevertheless, requests alone don't suffice. One must demand the redemption in the same way that an employee demands his wages. The *halachah* is, unless he demands his wages, there is no obligation upon the employer to pay on the same day. We too must demand the redemption, for if we do not insist, we then render it an unimportant issue."

The Chofetz Chaim wrote an entire book called *Tzipisa Lishua,* "Awaiting Redemption," in which he describes at length everyone's responsibility in hastening the coming of *Moshiach.* In addition there is the *sefer* Chofetz Chaim on the Torah where, in *parshas Behar,* we find an amazing account of his nightly vigils to bring *Moshiach:* "Many of the people who were frequently visiting the home of the Chofetz Chaim witnessed the following: At midnight, when all of his family were fast asleep, and outside was absolutely quiet, the Chofetz Chaim would enter his study, close the door and not permit anyone to enter. No light would be lit. The room was in total darkness."

Chofetz Chaim's Nightly Vigil for Moshiach

Occasionally, a number of individuals who were close to him would stand outside the door and listen to the Chofetz Chaim pleading and pouring out his heart to God the Almighty. His words were sharp and clear. He began by offering praise to God for the kindness he bestowed, detailing every happening in his life. He would look at every detail as a great merit, thanking God for his kindness. When he finished detailing his own life, he began speaking of the merit of *Klal-Yisroel,* the Jewish people. At this point, both his style of speech as well as his tone of voice changed drastically. Instead of thanking and pleading, he began demanding. The demand incorporated a statement to God the Almighty that He owes His nation Israel a full accounting.

At this point he asked, "God, what have You given us? You gave us a great holy Torah, but it was sealed and closed. What have we done in return? We opened the Torah, gave you the prophets, the sages of the Talmud, the Torah geniuses, we tied crowns to the oral Torah. But alas, what have we received in return for this? We received misfortune, persecutions, and murder. We weren't prepared for this. Throughout the lands, we Jews were dispersed and exiled. We brought our Torah with us, carrying it with us, saving it from our enemies, and we carry it still to this very day! It's firmly within our grasp." This was the accounting. Now would come the demand for payment of the debt.

"How much longer must we wait? Until when? We are totally broken. God, consider and ponder, can You find the heart of one Jew whole?" Suddenly he began to call for help to all the *tzadikkim* of the generations that had gone to their eternal rest. "Where are you?" he shouted. "Why are you quiet? You are supposed to be the claimants for us! Holy Souls, have you already forgotten everything?" This is what the Chofetz Chaim would do every night. When the horizon became light, he would return to his studies, awaiting *Moshiach's* arrival, confident then that the debt owed would be paid.

Rabbi Yaakov Kaminetsky,
Leading Rosh Yeshivah *of Our Generation*

Rabbi Yaakov Kaminetsky, one of the leading *rosh yeshivos* of our generation, is quoted in an article printed in the rabbinical magazine *Oraisa,* Iyar 5743 (1983): "With great sincerity, the Chofetz Chaim imbued in the hearts of Jews the anticipation for *Moshiach's* arrival. Even the simple Jew was caught up with the spirit of hope that the Chofetz Chaim infused among the Jewish people. Thus, he revived the learning of the talmudic tractates that discuss the Holy Temple and its sacrifices. He introduced all this to the broad populace, and especially to the *kohanim,* for they would be the ones to perform the sacrifices. This underscored the learned sage's preparedness for the coming of *Moshiach.* We too are required to pine for *Moshiach* and prepare ourselves for his arrival.''

Seeing how Jewish scholars of all backgrounds— Sephardic, Ashkenazic, chasidic, and kabbalistic—agree on the importance of awaiting and demanding *Moshiach,* we can examine and understand the novelty that Chasidus has contributed to the concept of *Moshiach.* This contribution is not just philosophical, but very practical.

MOSHIACH—THE CULMINATION AND PURPOSE OF CREATION

As mentioned before, *Moshiach* is the culmination of creation. God created the world for a purpose. The purpose is for the Jews to make Him a home in this physical world. This home must include the entire world, from the inanimate to the human. God gave us a Torah to be the guiding light and blueprint for the building of His house. Why is it important to do this for God? The basic answer is because God wants His essence to be perceived all over, at all times. Therefore, all of the world must be involved. Torah says that when this house is built, this will be the culmination of God's desire.

On the collective level, this will take place when *Moshiach* arrives. *Moshiach* is a person of flesh and blood who will announce to the Jewish people that the "house" is finally built, and we are ready to proceed to the era which he will usher in.

In kabbalistic terminology, *Moshiach* will symbolize that the reunification of the divine sparks with their source, the Godhead, has been completed. Kabbalah teaches that when God created the world, divine sparks shattered the vessels and the sparks fell on earth to all of physical matter. When *Moshiach* arrives there will be the restoration of these sparks and the Godhead will once again be apparent. This we call *Gilui Elokus,* the revelation of godliness. So the concept of *Moshiach* is that godliness will be revealed to us in the same way that physical matter is observable and tangible. Since *Moshiach* is the culmination of God's intent in creating the world, it makes sense that all of the above-mentioned sources realized that just saying *Ani Maamin* isn't enough. Therefore they suggest demanding *Moshiach.*

In Chasidus Chabad there has been a positive revolution as far as the importance of *Moshiach* and its impact on being Jewish. Believing in *Moshiach* isn't enough, and even though awaiting *Moshiach* is of extreme importance, it is not sufficient. What needs to be done is to live with Moshiach by actually learning all areas of the Torah that discuss *Moshiach* matters, such as the Rambam's Laws of Kings, the Midrashim, and the words of our own chasidic masters.

SAYING AND DEMANDING *AD MOSAI,* HOW MUCH LONGER WILL WE BE IN THIS BITTER EXILE

Also, one needs to do all *mitzvos* with the intent that each *mitzvah* will hasten *Moshiach.* Finally, each Jew needs to sincerely say, "We want *Moshiach* now" and *Ad Mosai*—"How much longer will You, God, keep us in this bitter exile." In other words, Chabad demands that each Jew act as the Chofetz Chaim did, by speaking out and demanding *Moshiach.* In Chabad this concept is as important as *Tanach* (Torah, Prophets, and the Writings), Talmud, *Halachah,* and Chasidus. The concept of *Moshiach* is no longer a foreign issue—it has become a household reality. This we call "living with *Moshiach*" in daily life.

CHOFETZ CHAIM ESTABLISHES INSTITUTE FOR LEARNING LAWS OF HOLY TEMPLE AND *KOHANIM*

This approach to *Moshiach* is analogous to another practice of the Chofetz Chaim. In a letter (printed in *Igros U'Ma'amarim,* #110) to Rabbi Hillel Ginzburg dated 9 *Sivan* 5691–1931, the Chofetz Chaim responds to a letter from Rabbi Ginzburg regarding his trip to Riga to establish an institution for studying the laws of the Temple and the Temple services. This was called *Lishkas Kohanim.* The Chofetz Chaim elaborates on the importance of studying the laws of the mishnaic order known as *Kodashim,* laws pertaining to the sacrifices in the *Bais haMikdash,* Temple.

He goes on to say in this letter, " . . . if Eliyahu Hanavi and our righteous *Moshiach* come in our days, we will need *kohanim* who are knowledgeable in these laws in order to properly perform the duties in the Temple. However, not one *kohen* among us knows the laws of the sacrifices properly. What shame and embarrassment we will feel when *Moshiach* comes! We will have nowhere to hide our disgrace when it becomes apparent that we didn't prepare ourselves. Then it will be known that all our prayers and petitions that we recite three times a day in the *Amidah* and those we repeat whenever we recite the grace after meals ('May the Merciful One send us Eliyahu Hanavi . . . ') weren't said with truth and sincerity. For had we really wanted *Moshiach* to come, wouldn't we have prepared ourselves? This is analogous to one who had invited important guests to a feast but began preparing the meal only when they arrived. Wouldn't such a person be considered a fool? Besides the fact that his guests would belittle him, they would also criticize him for disregarding their honor by inviting them without preparing anything for them. This is exactly our situation. Several times a day, and several hundred times a year, we implore God to send us Eliyahu Hanavi, yet we do nothing to prepare for him!''

The Chofetz Chaim concluded his letter by saying, that due to his health, he must cancel his trip to Riga to initiate the Academy for *kohanim,* however, he asked Rabbi Ginzburg to show his letter to the philanthropists and other important people in the Riga community, who would donate generously when they saw and understood the importance of this project to the future of Judaism. We clearly see how the Chofetz Chaim emphatically believed, and more so, practiced the idea of "living with *Moshiach.*" Not only did he feel this way himself, but he demanded it of all his friends, supporters, and rabbinical colleagues.

TRADITIONAL AND CHASIDIC APPROACH TO
MOSHIACH

There is a story that I heard that highlights the differences in attitude with regard to the importance and relevance of *Moshiach*. A *chabadnik* was walking down the street. He met a neighbor standing at the bus stop waiting for the bus. They began a conversation, which got involved, and before they knew it they were talking about *Moshiach*. Of course the *chabadnik* was speaking about the importance of living with *Moshiach* in our daily lives. His friend didn't want to hear anything about it; to him it was insignificant. A while went by and the bus hadn't arrived. The *chabadnik* asked his friend, who was a Traditional Jew, "How long have you been waiting for the bus? And when is it supposed to come?" His friend answered the questions, but then he added that just as hair will never grow on the palms of his hands, so, too, *Moshiach's* and the bus's arrival will never happen, it's been too long of a wait, therefore they are fables!

The fact that thousands of years have passed and *Moshiach* has not yet arrived, does not imply that he is not coming. On the contrary, since we, today, have the merits of our ancestors, therefore we are prepared and ready. Also, it's known that the Chofetz Chaim would demand of God to send *Moshiach,* not just because of the observant Jews, but also because of the nonobservant Jews. They, he said, aren't guilty, they haven't learned, they are compared to young children who have been captured in war and grow up thinking and feeling in certain ways because they don't know any better. Also, the nonobservant Jews have been "captured" by a secular society that denies the existence of God and

Torah, therefore they don't know any better. And yet these ignorant Jews still acknowledge that they are Jewish, and that, in and of itself, is amazing and worthy of *Moshiach!*

Many Traditional Jews contend that the concept of *Moshiach* is part of Torah. However, since it seems to them so far removed from reality, some tend not to talk about it in a serious way, and definitely do not act upon it. It's swept under the carpet. Not that they don't believe in *Moshiach's* coming, they do. However, it's removed from their day-to-day life-style. The Lubavitcher Rebbe has recharged the notion of *Moshiach* in a down-to-earth way that's more accessible to the masses than the Chofetz Chaim's call for the study of the laws of *kodoshim* by the *kohanim.* That academy was primarily for *kohanim,* and the laws of *kodoshim* are very difficult. Therefore, even among *kohanim,* it was restricted to those who appreciated, and were willing to delve into, these complicated laws. However, Rabbi Schneerson's call to intensify our preparation for *Moshiach,* whose arrival is imminent, is one that all Jews, regardless of their knowledge of Torah, can act upon.

MOSHIACH'S ARRIVAL IS IMMINENT

In 1990, the Rebbe informed us that *Moshiach's* arrival is "around the corner." He quoted the Midrash, "your time of redemption has arrived." This was based on several factors. The Gulf War between Iraq and Kuwait was alluded to in the Midrash, as a war preceding *Moshiach's* arrival. The Midrash says that two nations in the Middle East region will wage war, and the Jewish people will be scared. So God says, have no fear, *Moshiach* is here, and he will announce "that the time for your redemption has arrived." There were many open miracles associated with Israel being saved from the Scud missiles. The fall of communism overnight, without bloodshed, was miraculous. The superpowers ending the Cold War and deciding to destroy nuclear weapons clearly attests to the prophecy that when *Moshiach* will come "swords will be beaten into plowshares." The historic events in the last five years clearly support Rabbi Schneerson's call for an active approach to allow *Moshiach* to come in through the "door."

MOSHIACH IS NOT A "CHASIDIC THING"

This clarifies the contribution that Chasidus has given to Traditional Judaism in regard to *Moshiach*. Now it's up to each and every one of us. No one can say that he or she doesn't know how to implement *Moshiach* as a reality in life. It's a matter of realizing that the idea of *Moshiach* has its roots in Torah, *Zohar,* Talmud, and Chasidus. The only reason not do anything about *Moshiach* is pure inertia, certainly not a Jewish value.

Moshiach was demanded by the Chofetz Chaim, who wasn't a *chasid.* Traditional Judaism avidly studies the Chofetz Chaim's code of Jewish law, known as the Mishnah *Berurah.* Most Traditional Jews follow his rulings in their day-to-day life. From waking up in the morning until going to sleep at night, Traditional Jews are willing to put aside their own opinions and go along with his advice. Why, when it comes to the essence of Judaism, God, and Torah, which is *Moshiach,* do many

Traditional Jews not only fail to obey the Chofetz Chaim's command, but reject and denigrate those Jews who are involved in actively bringing *Moshiach!* I say this not, God forbid, to speak ill of some Jews, but in order to make the point crystal clear and to awaken those people to the fact that active talking, demanding, and acting about *Moshiach* has the backing of Torah true sages, such as the Chofetz Chaim.

MOSHIACH WILL COME WHEN THE NEWSPAPERS WILL TALK ABOUT HIM!

It's interesting to note that the *chasidim* of Square have incorporated in the *Kaddish* prayer the notion of *Moshiach* as a reality. They say, *"viyekorev ketz mishechei"*—and bring close the end of time, which is *Moshiach's* arrival. Ordinarily, the text used by *chasidim* reads, *"viyekorev Mishechei,"* without the word *ketz,* which refers to a date by which *Moshiach* must arrive. In other words, it's not enough to speak about *Moshiach* from a talmudic perspective. That's important but inadequate. What counts is the incorporation of *Moshiach* in one's life as a reality. This reality expresses itself in the word *ketz.* Each time the *Kaddish* is said, *Moshiach* is immanent.

The Chabad *chasidim,* in addition to studying on a daily basis the laws of *Moshiach* from such sources as the Rambam's Laws of Kings, Chapters 11 and 12, have also brought the concept of *Moshiach's* immanence to the media and newspapers. This approach has its support in an anecdote repeated by the *chasidim* of Rabbi Schneur Zalman of Liadi, known as the Alter Rebbe. They would say in the name of their

Rebbe, "When will you know that *Moshiach* is here? When he is in the 'Gazettes'!" Recently, *Sixty Minutes* has had a full half-hour segment on *Moshiach* and the Rebbe. Isn't that a direct response to the saying of the Alter Rebbe?!

9
Self-Sacrifice—*Mesiras Nefesh*

The topic of self-sacrifice, also known as *mesiras nefesh,* for God, His Torah, and His *mitzvos,* is a topic in which there is a definite halachic, practical, and traditional view with clear-cut implications.

What exactly is *mesiras nefesh?* Simply, it's the act of giving up one's life for God rather than transgressing His will. The idea of *mesiras nefesh* is classified in *halachah* as part of the biblical *mitzvah* known as *Kiddush Hashem,* sanctifying God's name. It's derived from the verse in *Vayikra* (22:32) "and I shall be sanctified among the Israelites." The Code of Jewish Law teaches that there are only three *mitzvos* that obligate one to give up his life: murder, immorality, and idolatry. When a Jew is threatened with death unless he agrees to kill another Jew, or to worship an idol, or to commit incest or adultery, in all these scenarios, he or she is obligated to face martyrdom rather than perform the prohibited act.

However, with regard to all other *mitzvos,* there is
no such obligation. So, if a Jew is challenged, ''Eat this
nonkosher food, or else I'll kill you,'' Jewish law says
there is no obligation to allow oneself to be killed. On
the contrary, outside of the three cases, one has a halachic imperative to preserve his life.

THE HALACHIC PARAMETERS FOR
MESIRAS NEFESH

There are important exceptions to this rule. If one
approaches a rabbi and asks, ''Am I obligated by Torah
to give up my life for Judaism?'' the response would be
that it depends. If it is in private, he should commit the
sin and not be killed. However, in public, before ten
Jews or more, it depends on whether the one compel-
ling him intends the act to be done for his own personal
benefit, or whether his intent is to make him sin regardless. In the latter case only does *halachah* say to let him
undergo death and not sin.

This is all in normal times. However, in a time
of *shemad*—religious coercion—whether in medieval
Spain or Communist Russia, then even in private, and
even if it is for the oppressor's benefit or enjoyment,
and even over a minor *mitzvah,* one should allow
himself to be killed rather than transgress.

This is explained in *Sefer HaChinuch* by Rabbi
Pinchus HaLevi of Barcelona (*mitzvah* 296). Therefore,
the individual circumstances dictate the decision of the
rabbi to the question of *mesiras nefesh.* This decision is
of paramount importance, because the choice is between a *kiddush Hashem,* sanctifying God's name, or a
chilul hashem, desecrating of God's name.

This approach has its practical implications. When a Jew does any *mitzvah,* there is a certain amount of dedication required to achieve the *mitzvah.* This commitment is based on what Jewish law prescribes. Therefore, if *halachah* says one is obligated to put on *tefillin,* there isn't any room for debate. However, there are situations in which *halachah* itself says there is no obligation to perform a certain *mitzvah,* because of illness or some other reason. Here the discussion begins about whether to go beyond the letter of the law and do the *mitzvah* anyway.

We know that the previous Lubavitcher Rebbe demanded from all Jews, particularly from his *chasidim,* to have *mesiras nefesh* to disseminate Torah and *mitzvos* in Russia. This "call" was at the height of the communist regime, knowing well that the rulers were murderous and that informers were evcry where.

WHAT WAS THE LOGIC OF RABBI YOSEF YITZCHOK SCHNEERSON'S DEMAND FOR SELF-SACRIFICE?

Several questions need to be resolved. Did he have the right to require this of himself and his *chasidim?* Did he have support from the other rabbis? What, if any, philosophical strength did he muster to take this approach? Finally, did he not realize that he was not only putting his life on the line, but putting other people's lives on the line?!

Obviously, knowing the caliber of the previous Lubavitcher Rebbe, he was acting with *mesiras nefesh* and teaching Traditional Jewry the importance of serving God with *mesiras nefesh* at all times and all costs. The Rebbe was well aware of the halachic details concerning *mesiras nefesh,* but he realized that any lesser degree of self-sacrifice would, in the natural order of things, mean defeat for Torah and *mitzvos* in Russia and possibly the world. The Torah tells us not to rely on miracles when there is something we ourselves can do, and the Rebbe did all that he could and demanded this of others. His dedication to the inner will of God, that there should be a Jewish people revealing His presence, gave him the courage and strength to continue his mission in disseminating Judaism throughout Russia, via his emissaries. The details of the *mesiras nefesh* is recorded in *Likutei Diburim* (vol. 4, pp. 1218–1384).

This is the paramount contribution of Chasidus to the concept of *mesiras nefesh.* It is in these gray areas that Chasidus has shown the necessity of going beyond the letter of the law and doing the *mitzvah* anyway. Often the *mesiras nefesh* that Chasidus encourages isn't just the extra mile; it demands that one put his life on the line. It is this type of *mesiras nefesh* that makes the contribution of Chasidus vital for the very survival of Judaism.

However, before going into the details of this approach towards *mesiras nefesh,* it is important to demonstrate that the same concept exists within Traditional Judaism. Otherwise we are faced with the question of what gave Jews the right to give up their lives to build schools and *mikvos* in Stalin's Russia. If, according to Jewish law, one isn't allowed to give away his life for any *mitzvah* except the aforementioned three *mitzvos,* then what is the purpose of these hundreds of martyrs? Did they neglect the general principle of *vchai bohem,* and you shall live in them, meaning that Torah and its *mitzvos* have been given to us by God for the purpose of life? To understand this, it is necessary to mention a *halachah* from the laws of prayer.

HALACHIC EXAMPLE FOR *MESIRAS NEFESH*

The *halachah* says that there are two obligatory prayer services, those of the morning and the afternoon. They are mandatory, because they correspond to the two *tamid* offerings, one in the morning and one in the afternoon, which were sacrificed daily in the holy temple, the *Bais haMikdash.* What about the third service, *Ma'ariv,* prayed at night? Is there a corresponding sacrifice to justify it? The answer is no, there was no such sacrifice. This being so, is there an obligation to pray this nightly service? The code says yes. Even though there was originally no obligation to recite this prayer, the Jewish people have taken it upon themselves to recite it nightly, therefore it became obligatory.

To explain a little more, the general idea of prayer is a supplement to, and a substitute for, the actual bringing of sacrifices. As the prophet Hosheah says (Hosheah 14:3) *"unishalmo parim sifoseinu,"* "We will render the prayer of our lips in place of the sacrifice of bullocks." We aren't able to bring sacrifices because we don't yet have a physical *Bais HaMikdash.* Therefore, the Rabbis instituted that our lips and hearts substitute for the animals. This is done through the verbalization of words, which come through the lips but originate in the heart. This is the basic idea of *tefillah,* prayer. In light of this, the code says that Jewish people accepted upon themselves an additional service nightly.

This service, the code says, was initially called *reshus,* voluntary service. However, since it was adopted by all of Israel, it is now mandatory, and no Jew has the halachic right to reject this prayer and say, "I don't want to volunteer my time to recite this additional prayer, I have enough with the two others."

(The fact that the three daily prayers correspond to the prayers that our patriarchs Avrohom, Yitzchok, and Yaacov said during the morning, afternoon, and evening, respectively, gives support to the recitation of the nightly prayer. However, it doesn't mean that the nightly prayer was originally obligatory.)

From this *halachah* we see that something which was voluntary became obligatory. In talmudic terminology, a *reshus,* permission, because a *chov,* obligation. The question that must be asked is, how was one allowed to say this nightly prayer, since God's name is mentioned throughout the prayer? Isn't it considered saying God's name in vain, since one has no obligation to pray? What gives one the right to mention God's name when he isn't required to do so? The answer is, one has a right to say this prayer, which includes God's name, since it became the tradition of the Jewish people to pray nightly. So even though you weren't obligated to pray the nightly prayer, since it was adopted by Judaism, it now becomes mandatory.

In a similar fashion, even though there was no obligation to jeopardize your life for the sake of Judaism, regardless, Jewish people took it upon themselves to go beyond the letter of the law.

We can now proceed to delve deeper into the concept of *mesiras nefesh* from a Chasidic perspective.

NEFESH MEANS A ''SOUL'' AND IT ALSO MEANS ''WILL''

Chasidus teaches that the word *nefesh* has two meanings, ''soul'' and ''will.'' The second is not the conventional translation, but, as with all concepts of Chasidus, it has support in the ''revealed'' Torah. *Yirmiyahu* 15:1

quotes God as saying, *"ain nafshi el ho'am haze,"* my *nefesh* isn't to this nation. The commentators explain that here *nafshi* means "my will."

Chasidus explains that these two translations go hand in hand. The true expression of one's soul is his will. In other words, if the soul is truly involved in something, the will directs itself toward that thing. It is the indicator of who a person really is.

Therefore, if one wants to know where he truly is spiritually, let him take a serious look at what his desires in life are. It's not enough, from a chasidic perspective, to take a look at actions; it is the desires that establish whether one has reached an elevated status in his service of God. Actions determine whether one has reached his goals, but desires show what those goals are.

DOING *MITZVOS,* BUT FEELING THEY ARE A BURDEN

It's quite possible to actually perform the *mitzvos* while perceiving them as a burden. Performance of *mitzvos* can be dry, cold, and boring. As the verse in *Yeshaiya* (29:13) attests, "God says, since this nation has approached Me with its mouth, and has honored me with its lips, however its heart is far from Me." Their fear for Me (God) through the doing of *mitzvos* is superficial, it's an act emulating those who have taught them what needs to be done. They act by rote.

REB MOSHE THE *CHASID* AND HIS *DAVENING*

What does it mean to do a *mitzvah* with a "soul"? An example I witnessed is that of the *chasid* Reb Moshe Weber of Jerusalem. Reb Moshe had come from Israel to

Brooklyn to visit with the Lubavitcher Rebbe. I was asked by my *mashpia,* spiritual mentor, to bring Reb Moshe to our *yeshivah* in Morristown, New Jersey. That night there was a blizzard and the road conditions were horrendous. Reb Moshe asked me to leave a light on in the van. I didn't say it was dangerous or ask why, I just did what he requested. As I was driving, I realized that he was using the light to study the Talmud. I was very impressed.

We finally arrived at the *yeshivah* and Reb Moshe led a *farbrengen,* an informal gathering. It was special. I got a chance to see a living *chasid* who was meticulous about his learning. The next morning I observed him *davening.* His entire face was red, literally! He got so emotionally involved in his *davening* that the excitement was noticeable. It was clear from his face that Reb Moshe had been transformed to a state in which he had no concern about the time, the fact that someone was waiting to drive him back, or the terrible weather.

This impressed us even more than his learning in the van during the snowstorm. Learning is an act, something done with the mind, but it doesn't reflect who and what a person really is, or whether he or she is truly in love with God. However, when a person "turns on fire" during his *davening,* this tells you he is in love with God, no two ways about it. Reb Moshe showed clearly what and where his "will" was. Will shows the inner person, it "establishes the motive." Will is a mirror of the soul.

AN OX WITH A FUR HAT

We can now apply this understanding of *nefesh* to our topic, *mesiras nefesh.* Chasidus teaches that *mesiras ne-*

fesh is the dedication of one's will to God. In the terminology of the Mishnah, "make your will like His will." A story of the Baal Shem Tov and his *chasidim* illustrates this idea. The Baal Shem Tov was once with his students at the *Shabbos* meal, and asked that they each place their hands on the shoulders of the one next to them and close their eyes. They did so. After telling them to open their eyes, he asked them what they had seen. They said they had seen a vision of an ox dressed in *Shabbos* garments and wearing a *Shabbos* hat, known as a *shtreimal*, indulging in a *Shabbos* meal with passionate gluttony. They admitted they were bewildered. What was an ox dressed in a *shtreimal* doing at a *Shabbos* table?

The Baal Shem Tov explained that this was a Jew, a *chasid* wearing a *shtreimal*, who was eating his *Shabbos* meal. However, since he was indulging his passion for meat, his face reflected where his desire was, namely the flesh of the ox which was on his plate. A person is what his true desires are.

Mesiras nefesh means rededicating passions and desires toward the will of God. Chasidus cautions us not to attempt to become passionless and cold but rather to transform our natural will, so that the passion which is ordinarily directed to material things can be used for Torah and *mitzvos*. This gives us an insight into the *mesiras nefesh* of the previous Lubavitcher Rebbe and his disciples.

REB BERKA CHEIN: A YID WHO LIVED AND BREATHED *MESIRAS NEFESH*

Let me share with you two short episodes heard from Reb Dovid Mishulovin of Los Angeles, in which a Jew practiced *mesiras nefesh,* not for a *mitzvah* per se, but for the sake of chasidic practices. There was a *chasid* named Berka Chein, who was on the most wanted list of the KGB for disobeying their dictates and teaching Jewish children Torah during the Stalin years. His picture and name were widely distributed, and Berka had to hide indoors for fear that if he were to appear on the street, the KGB would arrest him and kill him immediately.

On several occasions Berka would tell the people who hid him that he needed to take a walk. The previous Lubavitcher Rebbe put great emphasis on saying words of Torah in public places, and he had mentioned that when one walks outside, he should orally review Chasidus and Mishnah, in order to "purify the air" of the surrounding environment. Berka took this teaching literally. If he stayed indoors all the time, he wouldn't be able to fulfill the Rebbe's instruction, so he went outside, knowing he was putting his life in danger.

Another story: Ordinarily, a *chasid* immerses himself in the *mikvah* every day before morning *davening.* One day Berka had a bad cold and wasn't feeling well. His hosts didn't want him to go to the *mikvah,* which was unheated. Berka couldn't accept this. He began banging on the table and demanding the key to the *mikvah.* His banging was loud and strong, and everyone present perceived that it was a life and death issue to him. For Berka, facing God in the morning without going to *mikvah* was out of the question.

For Reb Berka, going to the *mikvah* and reviewing Chasidus in the street were equivalent to putting on *tefillin* daily. There was no compromise! This is what it means to have *mesiras nefesh* even for things that aren't *mitzvos,* neither biblical nor rabbinical.

PINCHUS, A TORAH ZEALOT

The story of Pinchus is told in the Torah. Briefly, Pinchus saw two people cohabiting, one Jewish, one not, both leaders in their communities. In the face of criticism and physical danger, Pinchus didn't ask any questions and had the courage to kill them. The Torah promises that, because of his brave act, Pinchus and his descendents will retain the priesthood eternally.

The commentators ask, "How was Pinchus allowed to kill them without consulting with Moshe, the Rabbi and Rav?" They answer the question by introducing the legal principle of *halachah v'en morin ken;* even though the *halachah* is so and so, yet a rav will not instruct someone to do so. However, those that are zealous in their commitment to God will act according to the *halachah*. Therefore, Pinchus, who was zealous, acted accordingly, even though he knew that had he approached Moshe and asked him a *shaila,* a halachic question, Moshe would have been silent.

This was *mesiras nefesh* on the part of Pinchus. Since his will was truly united with God's, he couldn't allow the *chilul Hashem,* the desecration of God, to develop and become worse. Pinchus transformed it into a *kiddush Hashem,* sanctification of God's name, by killing the leaders and showing that God has the final say, regardless of the titles and honors of those involved. The bottom line is that God Himself announced that Pinchus preserved His honor.

RABBI YOSEF YITZCHOK SCHNEERSON, THE PINCHUS OF OUR GENERATION

Rabbi Menachem Mendel Schneerson, in *Likutei Sichos* (vol. 18, p. 318), explains how his father-in-law, the previous Lubavitcher Rebbe, was a Pinchus in his generation. He was steadfast in his approach to Judaism in Russia; he didn't run away, and he didn't tell his *chasidim* to close up shop and leave. Rather, he encouraged each and every one, man, woman, child, to have *mesiras nefesh* for Judaism. He demanded self-sacrifice of himself and his followers. He did not ask a rav if he was allowed to do so, but not because he was unscrupulous. On the contrary, because he had such a great love for God, Torah, and especially for every Jewish person, he put his life on the line.

For him, having a God without having Jews was tantamount to having no God. Therefore he acted just as Moshe did. After the sin of the golden calf, when God said that he would eliminate the Jewish people and make Moshe the father of a new nation, Moshe told God, "Erase me from your Torah"—If you get rid of the Jews, I go as well.

The previous Rebbe realized that locking up the *mikvah* and closing the cheder was equivalent to the destruction of the Jewish people. Therefore he went beyond all limits in keeping Jewish institutions open. And today, more than seventy years later, we see the results. Thousands of Jews were saved from assimilation because the previous Rebbe risked his life and instructed his students to do the same. This was a "Pinchus." He did not hold meetings and draft proposals. He got up and did what was necessary, putting all questions aside. True *mesiras nefesh* is a service of God that goes beyond the call of duty to the realm of absolute selflessness.

BEING A "PINCHUS" IN OUR FREE SOCIETY: LIVING FOR GOD, NOT DYING FOR GOD

It is crucial to point out that being a "Pinchus" in our day and age, in our free society, doesn't mean we need to martyr ourselves or live like prisoners in Siberia. One of the basic teachings of Chasidus is the involvement of the entire material creation in serving God. Self-sacrifice as an end in itself is a limited form of self-sacrifice.

We see this by comparing the *mesiras nefesh* of Avrohom the Patriarch to that of Rabbi Akiva. Rabbi Akiva throughout his life would say, "When will I have the opportunity to give up my life for God?" Rabbi Akiva's *mesiras nefesh* was limited because he had a certain desire that was independent of God's will. His will wanted to fulfill the *mitzvah* of *mesiras nefesh* through physical *kiddush Hashem,* which would enable him to reach the greatest of spiritual heights.

AVROHOM'S *MESIRAS NEFESH*

Avrohom had an entirely different understanding of what *mesiras nefesh* was all about. Avrohom understood *mesiras nefesh* to mean doing God's will regardless, including not giving in to one's own desire to give away one's life to God. Therefore he was prepared to do whatever God wanted. If God wanted him to die for Judaism, that was fine. If God wanted him to remain alive and disseminate Judaism, he was ready. This, Chasidus says, is the ultimate *mesiras nefesh,* the willingness to cooperate with God on *His* terms.

EVERY JEW CAN SAY, "WHY IS GOD NOT APPARENT IN MY LIFE?"

The Rebbe explains in his *Maamor V'Atoh Tetzave* (*Meluket,* vol. 6, p. 129) that every Jew can truly feel and say, "Why isn't godliness apparent in my life?"

When a Jew realizes that everything he has is worthless because God isn't apparent, this causes the individual to truly appreciate God and do His will. This, the Rebbe suggests, is the modern day *mesiras nefesh.* It's not jumping in the fire rather than converting to another religion. It's not allowing oneself to die or to be sent away to Siberia for violating the KGB's orders.

What is today's *mesiras nefesh?* It's incorporating everything in life for the purpose of serving God. This includes all comforts and conveniences. When Jews are able to do this, they truly are offering themselves to God.

In summary, the contribution Chasidus has brought to Traditional Judaism with regard to fulfilling God's Torah with *mesiras nefesh* include:

1. *Mesiras nefesh* isn't an external commitment, rather it's the dedication of one's inner desire and will. *Mesiras nefesh* is the pinnacle of a Jew's commitment to God.

2. The highest level of *mesiras nefesh* goes completely beyond the rational and legalistic. Therefore, asking the question of whether one should have *mesiras nefesh* is a limited form of *mesiras nefesh.* Every Jew is capable of more than this, as the previous Lubavitcher Rebbe showed.

3. *Mesiras nefesh* doesn't only mean to "do or die" for God. Primarily, it is the willingness to submit one's will to God's will in all situations. For the Jew in Russia, it meant not closing the shuls and *mikvos.* For his grandchildren and their contemporaries in America, it means feeling the same dedication for God, even amid our free society. In this situation there is an opportunity to serve God with all of the advantages of the material and intellectual wealth, high status, and politi-

cal influence that Jewish people have today. These things cannot be ignored; they have been granted for a purpose, and it requires *mesiras nefesh* to reveal this purpose and not succumb to the "test of affluence," which can be a more difficult ordeal than poverty. Avrohom, more than Rabbi Akiva, taught what *mesiras nefesh* truly means.

10

Deed or Study

This is an age-old debate, beginning with the two opinions in the Talmud (*Kiddushin* 40:2) on the question of which is greater, studying Torah or doing *mitzvos*. Of course, both are necessary; without doing all of the *mitzvos* or without learning the required amount, one isn't in the realm of this discussion. The debate concerns what the emphasis should be on study or deed. Or, to clarify the question, if one has some extra time after doing the required Torah study and the required *mitzvos,* should he learn or do *mitzvos?*

The Talmud concludes that learning is greater because it motivates action. Without Torah study one doesn't have the knowledge needed for practice, whether in terms of the details of the *mitzvos* or of the *aggadic,* stories, part of the Torah, which "draws the heart." This conclusion seems to imply that study is primary; given that spare hour, one should learn.

ACTION IS THE OBJECTIVE OF STUDY

However, a deeper analysis proves otherwise. Study is greater, says the conclusion of the Talmud, because it leads to action. Therefore, it is really action that is the objective, and this objective gives the importance of studying, since without learning proper action is impossible. Therefore, action is in truth the greater of the two. The same discussion is quoted in *Bava Kamma* 17a. Rashi comments that from the Talmud's words "learning is greater because it leads one to act," so we understand that action is greater, agreeing with the above explanation. Chasidus adds that when *Moshiach* comes action will be greater. It's only prior to the arrival of *Moshiach* that learning is greater.

This understanding, contributed by Chasidus to the talmudic discussion, is supported by the fact that the Talmud was studied and recorded in Babylon. The word *Babylon* comes from *bavel,* which means confused. In other words, the Babylonian Talmud allows for confusion, darkness, and questions, in the sense that one doesn't see the entire answer. In our context, the Babylonian Talmud writes that learning is greater because it addresses the situation before the coming of *Moshiach,* who will take away the darkness.

Chasidus, which prepares the world for the revelations that the world will experience when *Moshiach* comes, teaches that action is greater. Until *Moshiach* comes, study is greater because it is needed in a world of confusion and darkness. The light shed by study dispels some of this darkness and enables the performance of *mitzvos.* However, when *Moshiach* comes and everything is clear and obvious, action will not depend upon study, and action will be greater.

THE ULTIMATE OBJECTIVE OF CREATION

Chasidus uses an analogy from *Shabbos.* The Friday-night prayer states that *Shabbos* was "last in action but first in thought." Even though it's the last day of the week, it's what God wanted first, prior to the six days of creation. The purpose of the first six days is the *Shabbos,* but God made His world in such a way that in order to appreciate *Shabbos,* one must prepare himself during the preceding six days. In the same vein, it's impossible to have deed without study, even if the deed is the objective.

A more simple example: When one wants to build a house, one hires an architect to draw the plans of where each room will be, and how each room will be finished. However, it is a long process from this stage until the actual painting and carpeting of the rooms. In fact, many times the plans are ready but there is no money to buy the materials to implement them. Eventually, money is found, but there is no contractor available to do the actual building. Even after the house is built, the building inspector may not approve that everything is up to code, sound, and safe. Finally, after all this it is possible to move in to the home, after months and years of time, energy, and money.

THE SPIRITUAL HOME OF GOD

Metaphorically speaking, God's desire is the home with all of its rooms nicely "painted and carpeted." However, in order to accomplish this, a Jew needs the plans, which are in the Torah, "the blueprint of the world." After that he needs to acquire the materials and erect the building. This is the concept of *mitzvos*, action, not just plans. This isn't enough, because it's quite possible that one's building lacks strong materials and is not a safe, sturdy construction. Until the chief inspector comes and approves the home, no one can actually move in.

This corresponds to the idea that without God's approval, one has no guarantee that his building is what God wants. It is possible that the person is fooling himself, and he should be building something else. How does one ultimately know whether or not he is doing what God wants? Maybe he is confusing his true mission in life?

The only one who can say without a doubt that a Jew is doing what he or she is supposed to is Hashem, as He communicates through his Torah. He is the "inspector." It's only after these steps that the "home" is ready.

HIDDUR MITZVAH, THE EXTRA CARE AND ATTENTION WHEN DOING A *MITZVAH*

An important area in which we can see a difference of opinion in regard to what should be the emphasis, deed or study, is *hiddur mitzvah,* how one takes pains to beautify the *mitzvos.*

For example, take the *mitzvah* of *tzitzis.* According to most authorities, in order to fulfill the *mitzvah* of *tzitzis,* one should wear a woolen garment that has woolen *tzitzis.* There are a few authorities that rule that a cotton garment with woolen *tzitzis* is sufficient. I have seen many fine religious people wearing the cotton garment and asked them, "Why do you follow the lenient opinion?'' The response has been that since it's very hot outside, they don't want the woolen garment to become sweaty and thereby disgrace the *mitzvah.* On the other hand, with a cotton garment, they won't perspire as much, there will be no bad smell, and it won't dishonor the *mitzvah* of *tzitzis.*

In Chabad chasidic circles, this excuse is not heard of. The reason why the *chabadnik* won't say this is because he knows and believes that it is impossible for a *mitzvah* to become a disgrace because you're following what it says in the Code of Jewish Law! If there is a problem, he follows the ruling of the code that a Torah scholar should have clean garments, and either wash the woolen garment regularly or have a second one.

This difference is based on what is primary, deed or study. The Traditional Jew puts the emphasis on study. Therefore, one should study the laws of *tzitzis* with all of the commentaries. However, when it comes to practice, avoid the extra effort and expense in making sure the *mitzvah* doesn't become a disgrace by finding an easy way to do it, even if this prevents him from doing it in the best possible way. On the other hand, the *chasid* says, action speaks for itself. Therefore, every chasidic *bar mitzvah* boy knows as a simple matter of fact that he will wear a woolen garment in one-hundred-degree weather!

DO NOT LOOK FOR EXCUSES AND WAYS OUT

To put it in another way, the *chasid* won't look to find a way out, even if he can justify it by finding a *heter,* a justification. This brings us to the other distinction, the concept of *hiddur mitzvah,* beautifying *mitzvos.*

Chasidim are very meticulous when it comes to the purchasing of items for *mitzvah* purposes. For instance, *chasidim* will buy large *tefillin,* and they will make sure to have the nicest *lulav* and *esrog.* The reason for this is the emphasis on deed. Many Traditional Jews, extremely careful about *mitzvahs,* don't make it their business to buy large *tefillin* or the nicest *menorah,* the philosophy being that the primary emphasis is on Torah study.

Both approaches are Torah approaches, both have their merit. It's up to the reader to consult his own *neshomah.*

11

Tefillah, Prayer

Another area of Jewish experience in which the casual observer can see a big difference between the traditional and chasidic views is that of prayer, known as *davening* or *tefillah*. Let me make it clear from the outset that all Jews who believe God's Torah to be divine *daven* three times daily. But it is nevertheless worthwhile to compare the chasidic ideology of *tefillah* with the prevailing attitudes of today's nonchasidic "*yeshivah* world."

WHY DO WE PRAY?

The Rambam, at the beginning of the laws of *tefillah,* states that a Jew is commanded by God to pray to Him. This isn't limited to times when there are problems, God forbid. Rather, prayer is constant. We need God to show us His mercies and grant us our daily needs. If God were to refrain, for just one day, from providing us with food, clothing, and our other necessities, we would start getting very uncomfortable. But human nature is such that many people begin realizing that God is in control only after illness or some other catastrophe. This realization prompts them to beseech God to continue providing them their needs. If they let the catastrophe serve its purpose, the experience can bring them to realize that prayer shouldn't be the last resort. It is better to rely on His mercies and to be thankful at all times, especially good times.

The Traditional Jew finds comfort in this approach to prayer. To quote the Rambam in his *Guide for the Perplexed* (Part 3, Chapter 36), "We are told to offer up prayers to God, in order to establish firmly the true principle that God takes notice of our ways, that He can make them successful if we serve Him, or disastrous if we disobey Him; that success and failure are not the results of chance or accident." The Traditional Jew believes in this more than 100 percent. He *davens* three times daily, every day of the year, plus all of the special prayers for *Shabbos* and holidays. He doesn't question or challenge the repetitive nature of prayer.

In fact the Traditional Jew is very particular about *davening* early in the morning, prior to the various deadlines associated with *zeman tefillah,* the timing of *davening,* as prescribed by our holy sages. The prayers are said not just with the basic knowledge of the meaning of the words, but more so, with *kavanah,* focused concentration on connecting to God through the prayers.

TEFILLAH MEANS TO JUDGE

Chasidus perceives *davening* in an innovative way. In addition to the requirements outlined above, *davening* has a much deeper meaning for the Jew. *Tefillah* is commonly translated as prayer. However, to pray means to beg, beseech, or implore, which have other equivalents in the Hebrew language. The word *tefillah* is more specific, coming from the Hebrew word *pilel,* meaning to judge. The basic idea of *tefillah* is that one must judge himself during *davening*. As he reflects on the fact that he might not be worthy of God's kindness and goodness, he acquires humility, which is the fit vessel for God's benevolence, for, as the Talmud says, God cannot dwell together with a proud person.

SECOND LEVEL OF *TEFILLAH* IS AVODAH, SERVICE

The second level of *tefillah* is *avodah,* service. This refers to *davening* as a means to change oneself. In order to truly connect with God, it is necessary to be a dedicated servant, in the sense of exchanging one's personal desires for God's desires. When one meditates on the greatness of God, he becomes inspired with the desire to serve Him. In this context, character flaws, based as they are upon unthinking selfishness, have no place, and a person is drawn to a higher standard for himself.

This *davener* is known as an *oved* and what he does is *avodah,* both related to the phrase *ibud oros,* the process of making animal hides fit to use. The tanner takes the outside of an animal and makes fine leather. He works on the raw hide until it becomes a beautiful piece of leather, perhaps even fit for a *Sefer Torah,* a Torah scroll. In the same way, an *oved* can labor to make himself into something which can fully express the attributes of his Creator.

Even though the materials used in the process may give him an unpleasant smell, it is all worth it. To hold the finished product in his hands, knowing that it took many hours of effort, is of paramount importance to the tanner, and the same is true for the *oved*. Yes, when one *davens* properly it takes time and effort. Even more, it is uncomfortable to take note of one's small-mindedness and corporeality. However, remembering the objective, the transformation of character, one lets go and jumps in with joy and anticipation. This is the second level of *davening* from a chasidic perspective.

HIGHEST LEVEL OF *TEFILLAH* IS *TOFEL*, ATTACHMENT AND BONDING

Finally, the third and greatest idea of *davening* from a chasidic perspective is the concept of *tefillah* as a bonding of the *neshomah* with God. Here the word *tefillah* relates to the Hebrew word *tofel,* as in the phrase, *hatofel kli cheres,* one who repairs a vessel. Just as two pieces of a broken container can be pieced together to make it whole again, the *neshomah,* with its godly essence, can be reunited with God. During *davening,* it attaches itself to God spirit to spirit, essence to essence. This is not about character change, or judging oneself; it is beyond all this. It expresses the pure essence of one's *neshomah* that only desires God and nothing else. This idea of *davening* follows logically after the first two ideas mentioned earlier.

DAVENING—THE FOUNDATION OF TORAH STUDY

A *chasid* perceives the importance of *davening* not just as another requirement of Torah law but as the foundation that enables one to study Torah the way it can and should be studied. In chasidic circles, philosophical emphasis is placed on *davening* more than on learning, because the importance of learning can only be appreciated through sensitivity and respect for God. Without this foundation, why should one really study Torah day and night? It can be much more interesting to study all kinds of "worldly wisdom" than to fathom the meaning of a three-thousand-year-old book! However, when one takes *davening* seriously, one realizes how Torah is fresh, new, and vital.

This idea is no secret. The morning blessings include a *berachah,* blessing, on the study of Torah, and the code of Jewish law specifies that it is forbidden to learn any Torah prior to saying this blessing. Why? Because this blessing reminds a Jew that the Torah one will study throughout the day comes from God, and therefore one must have humility and respect for the Giver of the Torah. Therefore, as the day progresses, when one has to choose between the Torah's opinion and one's own interpretations, he puts aside his understanding and submits to God's will and wisdom.

SPIRITUAL MEANING OF THE BLESSING MADE PRIOR TO LEARNING TORAH

This concept is explained in Rabbeinu Nisim on Tractate *Nedarim* (81:1) in the name of Rabbeinu Yona, and it is also mentioned in the commentator, Bach, on the Code of Jewish Law (vol. 1, Chap. 47). The Talmud in Tractate *Nedarim* studies the verse in *Yirmiyahu* (9:11, 12), "Why was the land destroyed . . . because you have forsaken my Torah." Why such a severe punishment? Rabbeinu Yona explains that surely the Jewish people learned Torah, but what was lacking in their Torah learning was saying the blessing prior to the actual learning.

Therefore, specifically because they were very learned in Torah, they received such a severe punishment. They knew better, yet they would not study Torah without pride and arrogance. In Rabbeinu Yonah's words, "The sages and prophets couldn't understand why the Jews were being punished until God Himself proclaimed, 'because I [God] know what their inner thoughts truly are, they didn't make the blessing prior to their Torah learning.' " Rabbeinu Yona explains this to mean that the Jews didn't study the Torah *lishma,* with the attitude that Torah is holy. Rather, they learned Torah routinely, as mental stimulation, and displayed their attitude by neglecting the blessing.

What this teaches us is that one cannot begin learning Torah without saying the blessing first, the blessing being the indispensable recognition that Torah isn't just another intellectual book but is divine revelation. That's where it begins and that's where it ends. The blessing also crystallizes the association between the giver of Torah, God, and the receiver, the Jew. By saying the blessing prior to the actual study, one draws down the essence of God into the Torah that is being learned. Without the blessing, what's missing in the learning of Torah is God's involvement, even though it is God's Torah.

The reason God isn't there is because He doesn't dwell in a place of arrogance. In the same vein, without *davening* as the foundation for Torah study, one cannot properly connect with God, because there is a certain arrogance that is natural to all human beings. It is only through the *avodah* of *davening* that one is able to remove one's pride and sensitize oneself so that the Torah study will be selfless, not selfish.

DAVENING: THE PRELUDE TO LEARNING AND THE WORKING DAY

We find a verse in the Book of *Yeshayahu* (2:22) that teaches us how *davening* is the absolute prelude for one's learning of Torah and involvement with all physical matter during the day. It says, "Stay away from the person who has his soul in his nostrils, for what (*bameh*) is he worth." The Talmud in Tractate *Berachos* (14a) tells us not to read the Hebrew letters *bais, mem* and *heh* as *bameh,* which means "for what," but rather the letters should be read *bomoh,* meaning a high place. In talmudic terminology, a *bomoh* refers to the bringing of sacrifices on a high and prominent rocky place. Before the establishment of the Temple in Jerusalem, one was allowed to bring sacrifices on such a high place.

Chasidus explains the idea of a *bomoh* in spiritual terms. Prior to *davening,* a person's natural tendencies cause him to be the center of the universe in his own eyes, a *bomoh.* This is also the meaning of the words in the verse, "his soul is in his nostrils," meaning that, prior to *davening,* the soul has not permeated the body and stands at the gate, the nostrils. He is, in effect, a newborn child wearing adult clothing, his vital functions confined to breathing and screaming! However, *davening* internalizes a feeling of humility and modesty, the foundation for a Torah-true life throughout the day.

This foundation enables him to learn Torah as it should be learned, as a search for truth, not an exercise in making one's own point of view prevail. After his learning, he proceeds to his work and elevates the environment around him. The positive impact he makes on everyone and everything comes naturally, because he prepared himself during his *davening* and the learning that followed it. An impression of his *davening* walks around with him all day, recognizable wherever he may be, like a shadow.

THE REPETITION OF *AMIDAH* DURING THE *MINCHAH* SERVICE IN LITHUANIAN *YESHIVOS*

We see a difference between traditional and chasidic *yeshivos* in regard to *davening.* In many traditional *yeshivos,* whose philosophy comes from the Lithuanian approach, during the weekday *minchah,* afternoon service, the one leading the service does not repeat the *Amidah* aloud. I asked several prominent rabbis and *rosh yeshivos,* deans, about this practice.

They told me that this was instituted by the great *rosh yeshivos* of our generation, and that the reason for this behavior is because the leaders of the *yeshivos* didn't want the students to waste time listening to the repetition of the *Amidah,* the blessings said silently, by the leader. After all, according to the Code of Jewish Law, it is repeated for the sake of those who are ignorant and can't read it themselves. Therefore, since all the students know how to read, it's better that they immediately return to their Talmud study after they respond to the *kedushah* (a responsive prayer required to be said by everyone present in the synagogue), and not to be involved in *bittul Torah,* subtracting of time from Torah

study, by just listening to the repetition of the *Amidah*
as said by the *chazan,* cantor.

THE REPETITION OF THE *AMIDAH*
IN CHASIDIC *YESHIVOS*

In chasidic *yeshivos* this practice isn't acceptable. On
the contrary, all students are encouraged to listen atten-
tively to the *chazan's* repetition of the *Amidah.* Part of
the philosophical importance attributed to this so-
called waiting period is the consideration one needs to
give for another Jew who is less knowledgeable than
oneself. Practically speaking, there are often plenty of
Jews who do *daven* with the *yeshivah minyan* and
don't know how to read appropriately. Therefore it is in
line with *halachah* to repeat the *Amidah,* even if it
were to be for the uneducated.

However, in addition to this pragmatic reason,
there is another reason that would require the *yeshivah*
students to listen and follow the *Amidah* repetition and
not consider it a pure waste of time that could be used
for more important things, namely studying another
page of Talmud. It used to be that many Jews were
ignorant and could not read Hebrew; therefore the
Rabbis instituted the repetition of the *Amidah* for their
benefit. Today, even though the majority of Traditional
Jews know how to read Hebrew, a majority, including
the most learned *yeshivah* students, aren't able to concentrate appropriately during their own saying of the
Amidah. Therefore, a most auspicious time to reflect
on what one has just read is during the repetition.
During that time one can take his time and focus on

what is being said, adding to one's connectedness with God through *davening*

A CHASIDIC *DAVENING*: LEARNING CHASIDUS, MEDITATION, FERVOR, *GARTEL*

At this point let us mention several innovations of Chasidus, which can be, and have been, adopted by many Traditional Jews. The first is what is called by *chasidim davening b'arichus,* meaning *davening* slowly, preceded by "thinking Chasidus." This may take several hours. During the *davening,* one meditates on God's greatness. Chasidic meditation takes a very thoughtful approach, beginning with learning Chasidus until the information learned is clear, storing it in one's mind, and proceeding to contemplate this data. These three steps are necessary for one to even consider *davening b'arichus.* Because all this takes time, many *chasidim* begin with the *minyan* but finish much later than the other participants. The reason is that they are *davening b'arichus,* and the others aren't.

ZMAN TEFILLAH AND *KRIAS SHEMA*, THE TIME DEADLINE FOR THE *SHEMA* AND THE *AMIDAH*

Chasidim have been criticized and accused of not reading the *Shema* and *Amidah* by the time deadlines prescribed by the sages. Let me say clearly and unequivocally that a true committed *chasid* doesn't miss the time for *Shema* and is credited for the saying of the *Amidah* in time, even though sometimes the actual reciting of the *Amidah* may be after the deadline. However, as will be explained shortly, there is an halachic basis for this behavior.

First, *chasidim* get up prior to the end of the time allotted for the saying of *shema,* and read the *Shema,* fulfilling their obligation. This way the *chasid* doesn't have to be concerned that he will miss the time deadline, because he has already said the *Shema.* Otherwise he would suffer anxiety, which would distract him from his *davening.*

REB CHAIM BRISKER'S VIEW OF *TEFILLAH* WITH *KAVANAH,* INTENT

What about the saying of the *Amidah* on time? It would seem that in many chasidic synagogues there is no care given to this important issue! To address, this, there is an important explanation by Reb Chaim Brisker, a great-great-grandson of the Vilna Gaon, who himself wasn't a *chasid* but was very respectful of *chasidim* and Chasidus. In his commentary on the Rambam (Laws of *Tefillah,* Chapter 4:15) he says, "If a person's heart is occupied with all kinds of matters, other than having the basic *kavanah* that he is standing before God Almighty, and he goes ahead and *davens,* it is not considered the service of *davening.*" His explanation supports the Rambam's view, which is, "Any *tefillah* without *kavanah* isn't *tefillah.*" It is clear from Reb Chaim and the Rambam that one must have the basic intent prior to *tefillah,* that one is standing before God about to *daven.* Without this *kavanah,* one's *davening* isn't *davening.*

Based on this, if one isn't able to attain this feeling within the time limit set by our sages, should he *daven* anyway? I believe the answer is no, because it's not *davening*. Therefore, many *chasidim* who get up very early in the morning, many hours before the last time for the saying of the *Amidah, daven* past the time deadline for the *Amidah* because it takes them many hours to attain this basic *kavanah,* which is necessary for *tefillah* to be considered *tefillah*.

The issue of *davening b'arichus* isn't emphasized in traditional *yeshivos.* As already demonstrated by the difference in the repetition of the *minchah Amidah, davening* isn't as important as learning. This attitude was initiated by the leaders of the *yeshivos,* because, as Rabbi Berel Wein says, the emphasis was on Torah learning, beginning with and exemplified by the Vilna Gaon himself.

CHAYOS, ENTHUSIASM AND FERVOR DURING DAVENING

Another important idea for the *chasid* during *davening* is the concept of *davening* with *chayos,* fervor and enthusiasm. In some chasidic circles this is called *hislahavus,* or as it is in Yiddish, *davenen mit ah bren, davening* with a passion. This involves external body movements known as *shukeling,* a Yiddish word meaning shaking. The verse that supports this behavior is "All my bones will praise you." For some *chasidim* the shaking is extreme, and for others, it is moderate. In addition to *shukeling,* some chasidic groups practice singing during *tefillah,* while others emphasize shouting the prayers. All of these different customs, and many more that we didn't mention, underline the idea that *davening* must be with a *bren,* a passion.

In Chabod circles the *davening* is generally quiet and unobtrusive, but very passionate and deep. This is because passion doesn't only mean external movement. It can also express itself in deep concentrated attachment, to the point that one might be totally glued to his *davening;* so much so that if someone tries to get his attention, there is no response, not because he doesn't want to respond, but because he didn't feel someone touching him. It is as though the person who is *davening,* isn't here, even though physically he is. Again, in Traditional Judaism this is often a nonissue. In fact, many times the emphasis is that the *davening* be calm and cool, without a *chayos,* fervor.

GARTEL, WEARING A SPECIAL BELT DURING *DAVENING*

Finally, *chasidim* wear a *gartel,* a special belt that separates the lower parts of the body from the upper parts, and most Traditional Jews don't. The law, as expressed in the Mishnah, requires that when saying the *Shema* one must make such a separation. In the days when people wore one long garment, a belt was needed. Since today we don't wear one long garment, but instead several different garments which create their own separation, why is it necessary to wear a *gartel?*

The answer is to outwardly proclaim this separation. In other words, halachically it isn't necessary. However, a *chasid* goes beyond the letter of the law and does so anyway. The *chasid* doesn't merely wear the *gartel* under his outer jacket, as some Traditional Jews do, but rather feels it is important to share the beautiful tradition with other Jews. Therefore, the *chasid* wears it on the outside of the jacket.

On the other hand, the Traditional Jew feels that since we have several separations anyway, why another one? True, the existing separations are formed by the usual clothes that we wear and therefore these separations don't stand out. However, the Traditional Jew feels that it isn't written anywhere in the Talmud or the *halachah* that we need to advertise our customs.

The answer is also that this is part of the preparation for prayer. A *pnimi,* a serious person, needs to prepare himself. The code stresses that a person must have a special recognition of God during prayer, as if the Divine Presence is directly in front of him. The *chasid* realizes that he isn't yet at the level of "a person should pray all day" (Jerusalem Talmud, Tractate *Shabbos* 1:2). He needs reminders. Therefore, by putting on a special *gartel* he fulfills the words of the verse "Prepare to meet your God, O Israel," and reminds himself of who he is praying before. It is a physical act that emphasizes the privilege of *davening* to God. Therefore it is worn on the outside, so that the person can actually see it and remind himself of God.

12

Education of Children

Jewish children are the future of the Jewish people. How are they to be educated? King Shlomo answers the question in Proverbs (22:6), saying, "Educate the child according to his way; even when he is old he will not depart from it." With these wise words, King Shlomo teaches parents and educators that what is taught should not only be valuable for him as a child but should also assist him as an adult. If the information will not be relevant to his adult life, it is not considered education.

THE EMPHASIS ON ADULTS

Based on this, the Code of Jewish Law enumerates the requirements that parents have in educating their children, in particular in the *mitzvah* of *chinuch,* education. However, in prewar Europe it seemed that children

147

were often overlooked in favor of adults. The doctrinaire rationalism of the time, which affected even traditional circles, made children seem somehow unimportant, since they could not hold an "interesting" conversation on the important issues of the day, most of which have been long since forgotten.

When little children, in all their innocence, asked difficult questions about God, the Torah, and the Jewish people, the answer was usually, "When you are older you will understand." The teachers failed to recognize the importance of giving good answers, or at least acknowledging the question as valid, resulting in literally millions of Jews abandoning Judaism and eventually turning to other religions for answers.

Traditional Judaism realized its blunder and decided to change. After the Holocaust, such movements as Torah Umesorah, Chabad-Lubavitch, and the *yeshivos* all caused a major shift in what should take priority. Judaism was being rebuilt with the emphasis on the children, and Jewish day schools opened up all across the United States. It was the children who would be the future leaders of our nation.

Most of the European scholars had passed on and there were no adults to replace them. The only possibility was the children. Notwithstanding the fine accomplishments of these organizations, there was still something lacking.

RABBI SCHNEERSON AND THE CHILDREN

This was the lack of personal involvement of the great Rabbis and *rosh yeshivos,* deans of *yeshivos,* with the individual children. Granted, the Traditional Jewish community had learned its lesson from the spiritual backlash of European Jewry, but there was not enough involvement of the Torah leaders in actually teaching and spending hours of their valuable time in educating the children. It took the foresight of Rabbi M. M. Schneerson to pave the way.

In 1980, Rabbi Schneerson called upon the children to lead the way in bringing *Moshiach.* He started the Army of Hashem organization. The purpose was for all Jewish children, boys and girls under the age of *bar* and *bas mitzvah,* to take the initiative in doing *mitzvos,* and learning Torah, with the intent of being living examples for their parents. The Rebbe started with the verse from Malachi (3:24), "to return the hearts of the parents upon (i.e., through) the children." He spent hundreds of hours talking to the children at special rallies held many times a year. It was clear to any observer that the Rebbe had made the children his priority.

The Rebbe called for all of Judaism to emulate his ways. He didn't claim to have a copyright. On the contrary, he wanted all great Torah scholars and *rosh yeshivos* to do the same. Thank God, today the Army of Hashem organization is one of the largest worldwide, consisting of over three hundred thousand members, all children. The approach that the Rebbe showed us by giving of himself to teach and inspire children is a lesson for all Jews who feel it is more important for them to spend their time learning than it is to educate the children.

The Talmud (*Yoma* 35b) says that Rabbi Eliezer obligated the rich to learn Torah. No one had more business interests than he did, and he certainly gave huge amounts to *yeshivos,* but he sat and learned like all the other students and was rewarded with success.

Similarly, who can say that he makes better use of his time in learning and developing the Torah than such *tzadikkim* as the Lubavitcher Rebbe? Yet he gave of that time to spend it with little children, speaking to them on their level and waiting patiently as his words were translated into simple English for those who could not understand.

ALL JEWISH LEADERS NEED TO DEVOTE TIME AND ENERGY TO EDUCATE THE CHILDREN

Therefore, the true meaning of "Educate a child . . . so that when he is older it won't depart from him" refers not only to the ordinary parent and teacher but more so to the person who is a talmudic scholar and desires to occupy himself with the secrets of Torah and to delegate someone else to deal with children. To him the verse says that only such a person can give the student and the child something that will remain with him forever. If he leaves the responsibility to someone else, the child might know the subject, but there is no guarantee that he will retain it as an adult. A Jewish leader does not just impart information; he gives over the essence of the Torah. This guarantees that the child will always retain that essence. "Even when he is old, it will not depart."

Chasidus has provided a living example of how the generations, regardless of vast differences in intellectual maturity, can unite. When a Torah scholar learns with a small child, they share the essence of the Jewish soul which transcends intellect, and the small child realizes that the whole Torah, in all its greatness, belongs to him as well.

13

Wearing a Beard

Another practical example of how Chasidism has contributed to Traditional Judaism is regarding the beard. Rabbi Moshe Wiener, who attended both *mir* (nonchasidic) and *Lubavitch* (chasidic) *yeshivos,* has written an exhaustive book on this topic called *Hadras Ponim Zokon,* a compilation of talmudic and rabbinic literature throughout the centuries, including the opinions and decisions of contemporary authorities. For details and sources, I suggest this book, but I will briefly touch upon some essential information.

TORAH SOURCES

A full, untrimmed beard is probably the most obvious outer sign of a *chasid.* In the traditional world there are those who wear beards, those who wear trimmed beards, and those who are clean-shaven. The Torah sources for growing a beard are based on *Vayikra* 19:27, "Do not cut off the hair on the sides of your head. Do not shave off the edges of your beard." Further on in, Chapter 21:5, the Torah says, "Let them not shave the edges of their beards." These verses are the basis for the prohibition of shaving the beard with an instrument that will remove the hairs down to the level of the skin. There are, therefore, many Traditional Jews who shave with something that will leave some slight stubble, or use a dilatory cream or powder, which is not in the category of shaving, even though it removes the hair completely.

Those who wear untrimmed beards, however, find support not only in these verses, but in others that imply a prohibition of removing the beard in general. The Torah says in *Vayikra* 20:23, "Do not follow the customs of the nation . . ." In *Vayikra* 18:3 the Torah says, "Do not follow [any] of their [referring to the Gentiles] customs." The Rambam, in his book of commandments (Negative Commandment 30), takes this verse as the source for the prohibition of following the Gentile customs, which is one of the 613 commandments. According to these decisors, since Gentiles remove their beards, if a Jew did the same, he would be in violation of "Do not follow their customs."

In addition, there are other halachic decisors who quote the verse *Devarim* 22:5, "And a man shall not wear a woman's garment." Since women don't grow beards, when a male removes his beard, they feel that he is emulating a women and thus in violation of "Do not wear a women's clothing." There are yet other verses in the Torah that are brought as support for the prohibition of removing the beard.

However, I am not going to argue the halachic side of this issue; that you can find in the book *Hadras Ponim Zokon.* My objective is to communicate the inner meanings associated with the beard or its absence, as expressed by great Torah scholars.

WEARING A BEARD IN THE 1930s AND 1940s

One of my rabbis told me about the following personal experience about growing a beard. He learned in Yeshivas Torah Vodaas, a nonchasidic *yeshivah,* in the late 1930s. All the students had shaved their beards, per the instructions of the dean of the *yeshivah,* Rabbi Shraga Faivel Mendlovitz. Only Rabbi Mendlovitz, who was very prominent and well respected, had a beard. In 1939, my Rabbi and some of his friends were sent overseas to study Torah in a chasidic *yeshivah* in Poland. After being there for a short period of time, they all decided to let their beards grow and stopped shaving.

World War II broke out, and they returned to America. As he walked the street of Brooklyn, my rabbi heard people honking their car horns at him. Initially he didn't know the reason; was he jaywalking? However, the people in the cars let him know quickly why they were honking their horns. They told him he looked like a goat by wearing his beard. Mind you, these comments didn't just come from Gentiles and nonobservant Jews; he also received this ''important'' message from many Traditional, observant Jews. In the 1940s one had to be insane to wear a beard in public. Not only was it unfashionable, it was considered an embarrassment to Torah observance. Yet he and his friends had the courage and strength to continue wearing their beards on the streets of American cities.

Why was there such opposition? Doesn't the Torah support this practice? The answer is yes, the Torah supports it. However, the attitude of those who scoffed was that the Torah wants a Jew to be a *mentch* among Gentiles. Therefore, when no one else was wearing a beard in public, it was considered not only a ludicrous act but a *shanda,* an embarrassment as well. They argued that in one room one can do what he likes, but in public, since anything one does affects the whole Jewish nation, he must act differently, hiding his Jewishness and looking like a Gentile. As the saying goes, ''When in Rome, do as the Romans do.''

This attitude wasn't coming from evil or ignorant Jews, but from very knowledgeable people, who themselves had studied in *yeshivos.* However, in the spiritually cold climate of America, they felt that certain things required a facade, and one of them was the display of facial hair.

HISTORY OF THE BEARD IN AMERICA

This ambivalence existed not only in the streets but in most *yeshivos.* In an article printed in the Yiddish newspaper, the *Algemeiner Journal* (May 26, 1978), Nissan Gordon gives another firsthand account of growing a beard in the *yeshivah* world of the late thirties and early forties. In 1920, Reb Avrohom Ber, who belonged to a chasidic group called the *Malochim,* originally *chasidim* of the third Lubavitcher Rebbe, came to America. He lived in the Bronx, and his home was an outpost for many *yeshivah* students. They would come to hear and experience a taste of old Lubavitch, dating back to the Tzemach Tzedek's (third Lubavitcher Rebbe) times in the middle of the nineteenth century. In 1938, the dean of Torah Vodaas (A nonchasidic *yeshivah*), Rabbi Shraga Mendlovitz, who made a practice of sending his students to various people to expose them to the many dimensions of Judaism, sent a group to Reb Avrohom Ber.

The group of boys who went to Reb Avrohom Ber were influenced by his words and deeds. One of the results was that they began growing beards. Upon returning to Torah Vodaas, they were asked by Rabbi Mendlovitz to leave the *yeshivah*. He explained that their beards would be a deterrent and that the parents of potential students would dismiss the *yeshivah* as being probeard. Nissan Gordon is quick to add the Rabbi Mendlovitz had a nice beard and was truly a God-fearing Jew, yet he felt that the survival of the *yeshivah* left him no choice. This was the predominant attitude in all American *yeshivos* of the time.

In 1940, the previous Lubavitcher Rebbe arrived in America. He immediately opened up a Chabad *yeshivah* based on chasidic teachings. Also, soon after the Lubavitcher Rebbe's arrival, the Satmar Rebbe, Reb Yoel Teitelbaum, came to the shores of America. Nissan Gordon writes that Rabbi Simcha Elberg of the *Agudas Yisroel* wrote an article stating clearly that it was Lubavitch and then Satmar, with their *yeshivos,* who made the wearing of a beard in America a daily occurrence. It was the *chasidim* who, notwithstanding criticism and laughter, paved the way, allowing the nonchasidic community and *yeshivos* to follow along. However, there still remained a large segment of the Jewish community and the *yeshivah* world who shaved.

THE BEARD IN THE 1990s

Since the 1940s things have changed. Today, in the 1990s, it is common practice among many nonchasidic Jews to wear a beard. There is no doubt that over the last fifty years, the overall impact that chasidic Judaism has made within the Jewish community has been the number-one reason why many Traditional Jews are wearing beards. In many Jewish communities throughout the world, the feeling is, "When in Jerusalem, do as the Jews!" Chasidic Judaism has opened the door and allowed the practicing of Judaism and its customs to flourish throughout the world in a public manner. The attitude of "a Jew at home, and an American in the street" has been diminished as a direct result of chasidic Judaism, and in many nonchasidic *yeshivos* you will find large numbers of students, regardless of their home backgrounds, wearing beards. It is the "in" thing!

What indeed is the reason that wearing a beard is so important, to the extent that people like my rabbi were willing to be publicly harassed and humiliated? As far as *halachah* is concerned, there are varying opinions on whether or not it is okay to shave. Therefore, one can find a rabbi who is of the opinion that shaving is permissible as long as it doesn't completely remove the root. So why put oneself on the line?

THE BEARD IN KABBALISTIC TEACHINGS

Chasidim cherished their beards for two primary reasons. First, according to the Kabbalah, the beard of a Jew represents great godly energy. In the terminology of the *Zohar,* "These thirteen *Tikunim* (connections) are found in the beard, and when a person has a complete beard he is called a loyal person, and all those who see his beard place their *emunah* (faith) in it.'' The concept of the thirteen *tikunim* is explained by the holy Arizal. Some of his explanation includes: ''. . . the attribute *rachum,* mercy (there are thirteen attributes of divine mercy, the second of the thirteen being *rachum*) is manifested spiritually, in the hair that grows above the mouth . . . .'' He goes on to show the correlation between the different areas on and around the face in which the hair grows and the divine thirteen attributes. In the language of the *Zohar,* ''There are thirteen places from which the hair on and around the face grow, and they are called the thirteen ornaments of the beard.''

This concept, found throughout kabbalistic literature, simply means that the thirteen parts of the beard are the vessels and receptacles for the blessing from above. It is the beard that is the vessel in which one causes the thirteen attributes of mercy to be directed towards the person, bringing him sustenance and all other good things. Rabbi Chaim Vital, the most prominent student of the Holy Arizal, says, ''Based on the words of the *Zohar,* one should reflect and realize how great a demerit it is to cut off any amount of hair from the beard, because all the hair of the beard is holy.''

A FULL, UNTRIMMED BEARD

The kabbalists are clear on the concept that it is the physical hair of the beard that actually brings the thirteen blessings of God's merciful attributes into one's personal and familial life. The *Zohar* and Rabbi Chaim

Vital don't say that only certain parts of the beard are holy. It is the entire beard, every inch, every strand. Therefore, the fact that according to the *halachah* one may or may not shave is irrelevant to the Kabbalah.

(It must be stated clearly and unequivocally that in no way, shape, or form is there a contradiction between *halachah* and Kabbalah. The reconciliation of the two is based on the different levels of understanding and learning of Torah. It is called *pardes,* which is an acronym for *peshat,* the simple explanation of the text, *remez,* the hints that are alluded to in Torah, *drush,* the midrashic homiletic explanations of Torah, and *sod,* the esoteric teachings of Torah. For an elaborate explanation of this concept, read the book *On The Essence of Chasidus* by Rabbi Menachem Mendel Schneerson, published by Kehot Publishing Society.)

Since we Jews are not just connected to God through the Code of Law but on an essential level, which is illuminated by the teachings of the Kabbalah, wearing a beard is of paramount importance. As I mentioned in Chapter 7, the Vilna Gaon, who is considered the father of the nonchasidic community and the genius of Torah, writes that anyone who doesn't study the wisdom of truth (referring to Kabbalah) isn't allowed to *paskin,* render an halachic ruling! What we see from the words of the Gaon, is that one doesn't have to be chasidic to adhere to the words of the holy *Zohar.*

Therefore, the issue of wearing a full beard, untrimmed from top to bottom, is something that is important to all Jews. *Chasidim* follow this teaching and because of it have allowed themselves public humiliation. They feel it is more important to draw down the godly energy via the beard than attain the superficial acceptance of people by shaving it. Once one understands that it is a question of choosing between God and mankind, there is no comparison. Some reflection on the general divine importance of wearing a beard makes it easy to wear the beard in the face of all obstacles.

EMULATING THE IMAGE OF GOD BY WEARING A FULL, UNTRIMMED BEARD

The second major reason that the beard is of paramount importance is the fact that man "was created in the image of God" (*Breishis* 1, 27; see also Ethics of the Fathers 3, 14). In practical terms, one should emulate the ways of God, and as much as humanly possible, have a Godly appearance. What makes a Jew look different from a non-Jew? It is his beard and his clothing. It has always been the custom of our ancestors to wear distinctive clothing, making it crystal clear that we are Jews. These garments were clean, respectable, and representative of the greatness and dignity of being a Jew. Likewise, it was and is the beard on his face that made him stand out as a Jew. This was always considered the *tzelem Elokim,* the godly image.

I recall Rabbi Elberg of the *Agudas Yisroel* giving a talk about Jewish pride and honor. He said that it was always known in the *shtetel* that the way a Jew dressed and the fact that a Jew had a beard made up the honor of God in the public's eye. He said that today many Jews hide their pride by wearing garments that are far from the godly image, and shave their beards because they are ashamed of them.

MESIRAS NEFESH TO GROW A BEARD DURING
THE HOLOCAUST

One of the first ways in which our enemies, throughout history, humiliated us was by shaving our beards. A Jew in his heart of hearts knows that being Jewish is the most important thing in life. Therefore, regardless of whether some people want to hurt Jews who wear beards, or humiliate them by honking their horns, this is our godly image and no one can be permitted to take it away. It represents the totality of Judaism; it is what our ancestors gave their lives for. There is a fascinating eyewitness description of the self-sacrifice of some Jews who did not shave their beards during the Holocaust. Rabbi Ephraim Oshry, in his book *Responsa from the Holocaust* (Judaica Press, 1983, pp. 5–6), records the following:

> The Jewish leaders were compelled to remove their beards for another reason. A special goal of the Germans was the destruction of the Jewish leadership. A beard was seen by the Germans as identifying a rabbi, and the Rabbiner were singled out to be hounded mercilessly and killed outright. The rabbis were consequently forced to remove their beards in order to protect their lives.
>
> Only two people in the ghetto retained their beards. One was the Rabbi of Kovno, Rabbi Avrohom DovBer Kahana-Shapira, who did not remove his beard because he was known to the Germans and stood to gain nothing by removing it. He therefore guarded the honor of Jewry by leaving his beard intact.
>
> The second individual was one of the important householders in Kovno, a *chasid* of Chabad, Rav

Feivel Zussman, who took the risk involved and did not remove his beard. He managed to retain his pride and glory for a number of years—until the "children's purge" on March 27–28, 1944. On that day the Germans searched every single attic and basement, cave and tunnel, in order to find the unfortunate children whom they dragged out to be annihilated. God! Avenge their sacred, pure blood!

A BEARD: A PUBLIC ISSUE

Are we going to give it up? Are we going to find loopholes justifying our insecurities? It is high time that all Jews come to the realization that wearing a beard is *the* practice that stands out it the public's eye. It tells the world that the Jewish nation is the chosen nation, even more so than sitting and learning Torah day and night! Studying the Torah is done in private; wearing a beard is a public issue.

Because of the significance of publicly displaying the image of God, all Jews, regardless of their involvement with the teachings of Kabbalah, should take another look at how essential it is to wear a beard—and not just a nice trimmed beard, which is not uncommon among Gentiles, but a full beard without any compromise, just as Rabbi Claim Vital instructs us based on the *Zohar.* Of course a trimmed beard is better than nothing, but the ultimate goal is the *tzelem Elokim,* a full beard.

ONLY THE VERY LEARNED
SHOULD WEAR A BEARD?

Even though many more Traditional Jews are wearing beards, there is an attitude prevailing among many nonchasidic *yeshivah* students that justifies shaving. They say that until one becomes a Torah scholar, one shouldn't wear a beard. It is the leaders of the nonchasidic *yeshivos* who encourage this behavior because it would be arrogant for a student who knows very little to wear a beard in imitation of his learned superiors.

The general idea behind this argument is alluded to in various places in the Code of Jewish Law. It is called *mechzeh kiyihura*, the appearance of arrogance. In other words, they claim that the truth of the matter is that the student is worthy of wearing the beard; however, since it appears to be arrogance, he should not do so.

I am sorry to say this, but to any thinking adult, the idea of *mechzeh kiyihura* cannot apply to growing a beard. If that were the case, one might as well not do many other *mitzvos* and Jewish customs, because one can always find people who will say that he isn't at the proper level for those good things. This is ridiculous.

In addition, wearing a beard helps the students to respect God with awe and to study better. The students won't walk around thinking how great they are; on the contrary, the wearing of the beard will instill in them a feeling of humility and commitment to God and his Talmud.

Here are some statements in the name of the Chazon Ish supporting the wearing of a beard for all adults and *yeshivah* students:

Chazon Ish, a Nonchasidic Rabbi and Halachic Decisor, Supports the Wearing of a Beard

Rabbi Moshe Sternbruch, the author of *Moadim and Zemanim,* wrote a letter to Rabbi Moshe Wiener stating what he heard from his teacher about the Chazon Ish, Rabbi Yehoshu Karlitz, a major halachic decisor of the nonchasidic community. His teacher told him that when a Jew with a shaven beard came to see him, the Chazon Ish almost regurgitated!

Rabbi Shlomo Cohen records in an article printed in *Digleinu* #79, November 1954, the following story: "Sixty years ago there was a meeting between the old Gerer Rebbe and the famous Rabbi Yerucham, the *mashgiach* of Mir, a nonchasidic *yeshivah*. The Gerer Rebbe had three complaints about the students there, one of which was that they shaved their beards. The Chazon Ish commented on the Gerer Rebbe's complaint, 'There is no good answer why they shaved; all the possible answers are excuses that aren't justified, and the students don't have any Torah sources to support their behavior.' "

Rabbi Dov Yaffa, in his book *Pe'er Hador,* says that the Chazon Ish was very upset about the fact that *yeshivah* students had justified the shaving of their beards. In fact, Rabbi Yaffa writes, "The Chazon Ish said that wearing a beard is not a chasidic custom, rather it is a paramount principle of Torah. A chasidic custom is required of *chasidim* only, but growing a beard is universal, because it is an *ikar*, a fundamental aspect of Torah."

HATAM SOFER'S RESPONSUM

Some rabbis who shave attempt to justify their actions from a responsum of the Hatam Sofer. But first they ask the following questions: "Does *halachah* mandate that Jews must have beards? Should rabbis at least have beards?'' One rabbi goes on to suggest that indeed there are two traditions, one pro beard and one pro shaving. He quotes the Hatam Sofer's responsum (*Orach Chaim* 159) as the advocate for shaving, making it sound almost as though the Hatam Sofer had a campaign to justify shaving! In this rabbi's words, ''Accordingly, the following comments of the Hatam Sofer should clear the air on this issue and provide a strong defense for the proshaving advocates.''

GERMAN JEWS WERE FORCED TO SHAVE THEIR BEARDS

When I read the responsum of the Hatam Sofer I was puzzled. After all, the Hatam Sofer was a great proponent of Kabbalah; how could he have written a responsum supporting shaving, which is against the tradition of the Kabbalah? Even though the Hatam Sofer says that ''all the sages of Italy shaved their beards and relied on the custom of Rav Menchem Azaryah [1310–1385], the patriarch of the *mekubalim,* who frequently shaved and was known not to leave even one hair [in his beard],'' notwithstanding these words, many Torah scholars, some ardent supporters of the Hatam Sofer's views, have said that this responsum was written at a time when many Jews in Germany shaved their beards. His community, although in Hungary, was generally part of the German-speaking world. Being a grcat *tzaddik,* the Hatam Sofer gave these people the benefit of the doubt by finding some support for their actions. This in no way implies that he advocated shaving.

The responsum of the Hatam Sofer and all the different ways of explaining it can be found in the *sefer*

Hadras Ponim Zokon (pp. 213–223 and pp. 629–641). After learning all the information pertaining to the Hatam Sofer's responsum, it will become clear to the proshaving rabbis that the responsum actually supports the opinion that shaving is forbidden. Since they have no other to rely on, what remains are the hundreds of uncontested responsa and other sources supporting the growing of a beard. This one responsum, which is highly contested by great Torah luminaries, is not at all adequate to justify shaving in the traditional community. So, in answer to the question as to whether Jews and rabbis must grow beards, the answer is most definitely yes!

At the very same time, a Jew who is God-fearing should give the benefit of the doubt to someone who shaves. This can be done by finding true reasons, based on Jewish writings, showing that those who shaved did so either because they didn't know any better or because of actual danger from hostile neighbors. Therefore, I empathize with those rabbis who are questioned by their students, "How is it possible to be a rav without a beard?" A possible answer is that for various reasons, one does not feel he has the strength to wear a beard. However, it is indeed essential for a rav, as for every Jew, and in time, with God's help, he will accomplish this as well.

14

Men Going to the *Mikvah*

Another area in which we find a distinction between Traditional and chasidic Judaism is the idea of men immersing themselves in a natural spring or in a *mikvah,* a pool containing at least about two hundred gallons of water, with various other halachic requirements. Let us begin with the history of this idea.

THE ENACTMENT OF EZRA HASOFER, THE SCRIBE

Ezra haSofer, the scribe, instituted the requirement that any male who has an emission of seed is required to immerse himself in a *mikvah,* prior to certain prayers and in order to resume the learning of Torah. Ezra's enactment was recorded in the Code of Jewish Law as a *halachah.* It was in effect as long as we had our holy Temple in Jerusalem. Once the Temple was destroyed, all laws pertaining to spiritual purity and contamination ceased to be effective. Subsequently, Ezra's requirement was no longer considered an obligation (though there are grounds to say that it still holds, in a limited sense).

CHASIDIM USING THE MIKVAH

With the advent of the Baal Shem Tov and Chasidus, the practice of men going to the *mikvah* took a different form. The Baal Shem Tov taught that even though we don't have our holy Temple in the physical sense, yet some of its rituals, spiritual in nature, should continue and even be increased. *Chasidim* began using the *mikvah* not just when required by Ezra but every Friday prior to the *Shabbos,* and even daily, as a preparation to prayer. *Chasidim* were taking on the idea of going to the *mikvah* with more joy and love then ever before. The reason was that since there was no actual obligation, it took a tremendous commitment. Going to the *mikvah* was coming entirely from his own desire. He truly had chosen to practice this.

DEPRESSION ISN'T A SIN, MIKVAH ISN'T A MITZVAH

There is a chasidic adage, "Just as depression isn't a sin, *mikvah* isn't a *mitzvah.* However, what depression can cause, no sin can cause. And what *mikvah* can bring about, no *mitzvah* can bring about."

There is no verse in the Torah prohibiting one from being depressed and down upon oneself. Notwithstanding, since during depression one feels helpless, one is able to engage in any transgression, because as far as one is concerned, it doesn't make a difference. His view of the entire world, including his own life, is dark and hopeless.

On the other hand, it may be true that for men to go to the *mikvah* isn't a biblical or rabbinic *mitzvah* in our day and age. However, the positive results from *mikvah* can be accomplished by none of the *mitzvos*. To understand how and why requires a deeper look at the philosophical and spiritual meaning of *mikvah* and, on the other hand, of depression.

TEVILAH, IMMERSION, ARE THE SAME LETTERS AS *BITTUL,* SUBSERVIENCE

In many holy books that explain the concept of *mikvah,* it is mentioned that the Hebrew word for immersion is *tevilah.* The way to use the *mikvah* is to immerse oneself from head to toe. If one's little finger, or even a hair, sticks out, it is not considered a proper immersion. Likewise, if any part of the body comes in contact with anything except the water, it is also invalid. The reason for both rules is that there is still some area of the body that hasn't been in direct contact with the waters of the *mikvah.* The interruption of contact between the body and the water is called *chatzizah,* separation.

Therefore, the primary requirement when going to the *mikvah* is *tevilah,* to immerse oneself so that the waters of the *mikvah* reach each and every part of the body. This concept is alluded to in the Hebrew letters of the word *tevilah.* When rearranged, these letters spell another Hebrew word, *bittul,* meaning humility and subservience. The idea is that when one immerses oneself in the waters of the *mikvah,* one is willing to dedicate oneself to God, that is, to submit one's will to the Almighty. Just as when he enters the water and allows himself to be completely covered, the same is true of the spiritual process taking place at that moment. He is allowing himself to be "covered" by the waters of God, meaning he is willing and ready to give himself over to doing God's will.

Also, just as when any item, regardless of how small and inconsequential, comes in contact with the body while immersing it is halachically considered a *chatzizah,* so too, if the person who immerses himself feels that in some small insignificant way he isn't able or willing to submit to God's desire, then his *tevilah,* from a spiritual perspective, is invalid. The reason is that he felt independent from God during the immersion; he wasn't willing to give in. This could be compared to immersing oneself in the *mikvah* while holding on to a *sheretz,* a halchically impure creature. In other words, while attempting to achieve spiritual purity by going to the *mikvah,* he is simultaneously bringing upon himself the antithesis of holiness.

Once it is understood that the spiritual purpose of going to the *mikvah* is to give oneself completely over to God, one can contemplate another, deeper effect of *mikvah.*

MIKVAH: TRANSFORMATION OF ONE'S ESSENCE

In a chasidic discourse given by the Lubavitcher Rebbe, Rabbi Menachem Mendel Schneerson, on *Shabbos Parshas Shmini,* 1956, he mentions the concept of *mikvah* as a specific cure for a certain spiritual ailment. This ailment is *Timtum haMoach,* the "clogging" of the mind, the inability of the mind to understand and relate to God regardless of emotional willingness. The advice given by Rabbi Shneur Zalman (in *Likutei Torah, parshas Torah*) is to do several things, one of which is to go to the *mikvah* before *davening* each day.

The Rebbe, in his discourse, added to this concept. He said that when one immerses oneself in the *mikvah,* he not only makes the transition from a place of impurity to a place of purity but more so, he is transformed by the waters of the *mikvah.* Since the *mikvah* is a place that embodies purity, when someone enters the *mikvah* and immerses himself he attains a new and fresh personality he didn't have before. Thus, going to the *mikvah* transforms not just a part, but rather the entire person in his essence. The Rebbe quotes the chasidic expression for going to the mikvah, *tunken zich in mikvah,* sinking oneself in the *mikvah,* as meaning completely submerging and being covered by the waters of the *mikvah,* to the extent that one's essence is "sunk" and submerged by God. Therefore he leaves the *mikvah* a new person. Ego and arrogance are no longer there, because the *mikvah* has removed them, as long as one connects to the spiritual idea of the *mikvah.*

USING THE *MIKVAH* DAILY

With a good understanding of what the idea of *mikvah* is all about, we can proceed to talk about the importance of going to the *mikvah* daily, prior to *davening.* In order for *davening* to be sincere and productive, one needs to do several things, one of which is immersing in a *mikvah,* to attempt to achieve the *bittul* granted by *tevilah.* When *davening* begins with a feeling of humility and subservience to God, it is naturally more desirable.

Because of all of the above, it is of paramount importance for the *chasid* to immerse himself daily in a *mikvah,* prior to *tefillah.* In fact, during the years in which the Russian government assigned KGB agents to find Jews who were observing Torah and *mitzvos,* some *chasidim* would risk their lives by walking the streets to find a *mikvah* in order to prepare to *daven* properly. (I heard this from Reb Dovid Mishulovin of Los Angeles, who had witnessed Reb Berka Chein, who was hiding in his home because he was wanted by the KGB, go out on a daily basis to the *mikvah!*) For *chasidim,* a community must have a *mikvah* not just for the women, but also for the men. Today, in many communities, a *mikvah* is available for men to go to every day. In fact, in certain communities there is competition between the different shuls. One of the ways a shul can entice people is by providing a nice hot *mikvah* on a daily basis!

TRADITIONAL JUDAISM AND THE *MIKVAH*

Most male Traditional Jews don't go to the *mikvah* on a daily or weekly basis as a preparation for morning prayers or for the *Shabbos* because since there is no halachic requirement, it is not considered necessary. The time that they do go to the *mikvah* is the day before Yom Kippur, since the Code of Jewish Law says to do so. Simply put, the Traditional Jew doesn't feel a need to connect with God through prayer by first immersing himself in a *mikvah.* Since his idea of *davening* is totally different from that of the *chasid,* it follows that going to the *mikvah* would be a waste of time. Instead, he could study another page of Talmud or *halachah*. From his perspective, he is absolutely correct. However, when one allows oneself to understand the purpose and meaning of *mikvah* on a spiritual basis, one will see the tremendous contribution Chasidus has brought to Judaism by encouraging one to immerse himself in the *mikvah* on a daily basis.

Now we have an answer to the question asked at the beginning of the chapter, ''Why and how does going to *mikvah* bring a person to the greatest *mitzvos,* even though going to the *mikvah* itself isn't a *mitzvah.*'' A fuller explanation is needed of how and why depression, which in itself isn't a sin, could lead a person to worse things than any sin can bring him to.

DEPRESSION MEANS BEING A SLAVE TO ONE'S SELF: NO FREEDOM OF CHOICE

Being depressed about one's transgressions prevents one from being a free person. In such a case one is captured by self-centeredness, a slave to negativity. This is the worst kind of feeling one can have, a paralysis leading to helplessness. With all other transgressions there is a means of escape; a healthy self that, if motivated in the proper way, will eventually change and begin to serve God again. However, depression denies the opportunity to change; the prisoner of depression can't unlock himself. Thus, even though technically it isn't a transgression of one of the 613 *mitzvos,* yet it can lead to what no sin can.

The other side of the same thought applies to going to the *mikvah*. Even though it isn't a *mitzvah,* yet what it can bring about in the service of God cannot be accomplished by any of the *mitzvos*. Why? Because *mikvah* unleashes the creative power of freedom within the Jew. When he realizes what going to the *mikvah* is all about, he internalizes it and is transformed. He becomes a truly free person and not a slave to his ego. Therefore, what *mikvah* accomplishes no *mitzvah* can accomplish, because all other *mitzvos* necessitate a feeling of freedom to perform them accordingly.

Without the *mikvah,* the performance of *Mitzvos* can remain very technical and boring, because one hasn't truly submitted to God. However, going to the *mikvah* is an act of giving the self totally over to God, which enables the performance of *mitzvos* with a true godly feeling.

All of the above should give all Traditional Jews a deeper understanding of what the chasidic custom is all about, culminating with actually going to the *mikvah* more often. If one goes once a year, let him go once a month. If one goes once a week, let him go each morning prior to *davening.* It will only bring goodness and true Torah greatness to one's life.

15

Cholov Yisroel, Milk Supervised by a Jew

Another area in which we find a significant accomplishment of Chasidus is in the exclusive consumption of *cholov Yisroel,* milk that was supervised by a Jew at the time of milking. In many places and times, people have utilized milk from nonkosher animals. Therefore, the Rabbis instituted that in order to avoid drinking nonkosher milk, one may drink only milk that was supervised by a Jew from the milking process on.

The Code of Jewish Law states that one should only drink *cholov Yisroel.* However, some people make the point that since those days have passed and people no longer milk nonkosher animals, there is no need for someone to actually make sure that the milk comes from a kosher animal. For instance, major dairies in the United States only milk from cows of a kosher species. It seems superfluous to require someone to drink milk that was observed by a Jewish person from the time of milking. Yet it is an accepted practice today in the majority of Jewish communities, where *cholov Yisroel* is readily available, to use only *cholov Yisroel.*

REB MOSHE FEINSTEIN'S RESPONSUM REGARDING *CHOLOV YISROEL*

Once it was established by the Rabbis to require supervision, the Jewish people have adhered to the rabbinic enactment and only consume *cholov Yisroel* products. This practice has been resumed by many nonchasidic Jews, who realize that the leniency practiced by previous generations was more a product of difficult circumstances than anything else. However, there are those who don't follow this practice and rely on a responum that Rabbi Moshe Feinstein wrote regarding *cholov Yisroel* (*Igros Moshe Yoreh Deah,* vol. 1, responsum 47). He says that in a place where it is very difficult to obtain *cholov Yisroel,* one may drink non-*cholov Yisroel* milk. Therefore, some people say that based on his responsum, it is permissible to buy non-*cholov Yisroel* products.

REB MOSHE SAID REGARDING NON-*CHOLOV YISROEL:* WHEN ONE HAS NO OTHER CHOICE

Since some people rely on this reponsum, it is important to take a good look at Reb Moshe's actual word. First of all, Reb Moshe's responsum was written many years ago when it was very difficult to get *cholov Yisroel,* even in the larger Jewish communities. Second, Reb Moshe says clearly that when one isn't able to easily obtain *cholov Yisroel,* one may rely on the *heter,* lenient ruling, that non-*cholov Yisroel* is acceptable. Notice that he only says "acceptable," not that one should just rely on the lenient approach. In other words, what Reb Moshe is saying is just the opposite of the way some have chosen to misconstrue his words. He is saying that the proper procedure is to only use *cholov Yisroel.* However, if for some reason one cannot get *cholov Yisroel,* one may then, and only then, use non-*cholov Yisroel.*

Third, in another responsum (*Yoreh Deah,* vol. 2, responsum 35) he clearly states that a God-fearing Jew should be stringent and only use *cholov Yisroel.* He goes on to say that in the *yeshivos* it is of paramount importance to buy the children only *cholov Yisroel,* even though it is much more expensive and the schools don't have the money. He explains that by doing this, one shows the children what it means to truly have fear for God and what Jewish education is all about! He says, "After all, this should be the desire and intent of the teachers, to instill in the children *yiras shomayim,* the fear of heaven." By buying *cholov Yisroel* when it is expensive and money is tight, the children see a living example of how to lead a Torah life-style. Here is a translation of Reb Moshe's responsum:

> In reference to the dairy companies in our country, which I explained in *Igros Moshe,* Chapter 47, that there is no prohibition of milk milked by a non-Jew that a Jew has not seen, still in all, it is appropriate for all *Baalei Nefesh* [people concerned with their souls] to be more stringent.
>
> For this reason, it is surely appropriate for directors of *yeshivos*—elementary schools—to serve their students milk from those companies who have Jews watching the milking. Even though this

[milk] is more expensive, which for the *yeshivos* will amount to a large sum over the course of a year, and the financial situation of *yeshivos* is tight these days, which for this reason certain *yeshivos* are lenient in this area, still in all it is worthwhile to be stringent. For this too is part of the education and learning process, that they [the children] should know that it is worthwhile and appropriate for a *Ben Torah* to be stringent even when there is merely a [slight] concern or prohibition. From this they will understand and see how important it is to avoid prohibitions. And all the expenses of a *yehivah* are to rear and teach a faithful generation to Hashem and His Torah. Therefore, when it comes to issues of *Chinuch,* one should never skimp.

But, in the distant areas, where there are no *cholov Yisroel* companies, and it is very difficult to obtain milk that was watched by a Jew at the milking, even individuals need not be stringent.

Therefore, it is time for all Jews to make a concerted effort to consume only *cholov Yisroel* and stop using non-*cholov Yisroel* products, since today, almost all over the world, they are easy to obtain, especially in the United States.

CHASIDIM SHOWED SELF-SACRIFICE IN USING ONLY *CHOLOV YISROEL*

For years *chasidim* have only used *cholov Yisroel,* knowing the many stories, beginning with the Baal Shem Tov, about the positive impact *cholov Yisroel* milk has on unborn children and nursing babies.

In addition, *cholov akum,* milk of the Gentiles, can also cause a person to have doubts about whether or not God exists, or whether Torah is divine. A father-in-law once came to Rabbi Shneur Zalman of Liadi and said that his son-in-law had these doubts. He responded that it was because his son-in-law was drinking *cholov akum.*

REB NOCHUM TZERNOBEL AND *CHOLOV AKUM*

There is a story that describes the importance of drinking only *cholov Yisroel.* Reb Nochum of Chernobyl once asked that a cup of milk be brought to him. After receiving the milk, he said to the person who brought him the milk, "Where is the milk?" The person said, "It is on the table right before your eyes!" Reb Nochum said, "I do not see it! His assistant said, "It is right here." Again Reb Nochum said, "I do not see it!" The assistant understood that something was not right. He investigated where the milk came from and found out that the milk was *cholov akum!* However, he still did not understand why Reb Nochum did not physically see the milk, so he asked Reb Nochum to explain. Reb Nochum said that the Talmud says, "Milk milked by a non-Jew, and a Jew does not see it [supervise its milking], it is prohibited for a Jew to drink it." So Reb Nochum explained the language of the law to be very literal: non-Jewish milk is not seen by a Jew; a Jew literally does not see the milk. Therefore, Reb Nochum actually did not see the glass of milk that was put before him because it was not *cholov Yisroel,* it was *cholov akum!*

THE ARUCH HASHULCHAN'S VIEW
OF *CHOLOV AKUM*

The Aruch haShulchan, who was not a *chasid,* presents a very strong opinion on this issue. He writes (*Yoreh Deah* 115:8):

. . . it [*cholov akum*] is forbidden under any cir- cumstances, and not like the opinion of one great *acharon* (rabbinic authority) who is lenient, and he brings proof to his opinion from several great scholars . . they do not realize that the words of our sages are more stringent than the words of the Torah. The *talmid chocham* [scholar] who does so, great is his sin, and since the *Tur* and *Shulchan Aruch,* (codifiers of Jewish Law) have ruled that it is forbidden, who has the *chutzpah* to fulfill their hearts' desire? Let the one who guards his soul stay far away from it.

More so, let me clarify how all the words of our holy sages are like burning coals. Once it hap- pened that a person came to me and poured his heart out by telling me how he and his friends, when they were on a business trip, would drink their morning cup of hot milk, which they bought at a store across from their inn. Once they decided to ask the storekeeper where he bought his milk. He said, 'From the Gentile butcher down the block!' This butcher had a special recipe for com- bining milk with (nonkosher) animal by-products to produce a 'coffee whitener.' This person came to me saying how wise the words of our sages are. Truthfully speaking, all the rabbinic enactments are supported by esoteric reasons that have not been revealed to us. The one who will listen (not to drink *cholov akum*), will find grace and blessing from God Almighty, and he will be repaid in this world and the world to come.

There is no question that *chasidim* have had to self-sacrifice not to consume non-*cholov Yisroel* during the times that it was nearly impossible to get *cholov Yisroel,* especially for those with little infants who needed milk. This *mesiras nefesh* has not only affected their homes and communities in a positive way but has also impacted many Traditional Jews to begin using only *cholov Yisroel.* All that's left is that all other Traditional Jews who for some reason aren't yet using *cholov Yisroel* should climb on the bandwagon.

16

Rabbeinu Tam's *Tefillin*

Another issue with which *chasidim* have been scrupulous is in wearing a second pair of *tefillin* called Rabbeinu Tam's. Rashi's grandson Rabbeinu Tam had an opinion that differed from Rashi's as to how the Torah portions within the *tefillin* should be arranged. Rashi's is the opinion accepted by all of Jewry. However, the Code of Jewish Law says that a true God-fearing Jew should also put on a pair of *tefillin* in which the portions of the Torah are arranged according to Rabbeinu Tam's opinion.

Chasidim for centuries have been donning this second pair of *tefillin* with great enthusiasm and excitement. Most *chasidim* begin wearing Rabbeinu Tam's *tefillin* after their marriage. However, since 1976, in Chabad circles, one begins wearing two pairs of *tefillin* at one's *bar mitzvah*. The reason for this is, as the Rebbe explained when he suggested that people begin wearing two pairs of *tefillin* at their *bar mitzvah,* that the world today has so much spiritual darkness that any positive Jewish custom or *mitzvah* that one can add to his daily life is good and praiseworthy.

SOME ARGUE: ONLY GOD-FEARING JEWS SHOULD WEAR RABBEINU TAM'S *TEFILLIN*

Most Traditional Jews still have not adopted this idea, which is clearly mentioned in the Code of Jewish Law. Their thinking is, "Who are we to consider ourselves God-fearing to the extent that we should wear a second pair of *tefillin*." Addressing this argument, there is another responsum from Reb Moshe Feinstein (*Igros Moshe, Orach Chaim*, vol. 4, responsum 9). He himself was encouraged by the Lubavitcher Rebbe to wear Rabbeinu Tam's *tefillin*. Reb Moshe responds by writing to the Rebbe that he would like to start wearing them again. He says he used to have a kosher pair, which became ruined. If the Rebbe can suggest a God-fearing scribe, he would be delighted to buy a pair and start wearing them again. And so it happened. Rabbi Zirkind, a God-fearing *sofer*, scribe, wrote a pair of Rabbeinu Tam's *tefillin* for Reb Moshe. He then began wearing Rabbeinu Tam's *tefillin*.

REB MOSHE FEINSTEIN'S APPROACH

Reb Moshe Feinstein didn't make any conditions regarding wearing Rabbeinu Tam's *tefillin*. In his responsum he says nothing about having to be a God-fearing Jew in order to wear Rabbeinu Tam's *tefillin,* even though the code mentions it.

It goes without saying that it sets a dangerous precedent to start discarding Jewish customs because "we are not holy enough." The truth of the matter is that after our experiences in the last fifty years, spiritually and physically we are holy and God-fearing Jews.

THE *ARUCH HASHULCHAN*'S ENCOURAGEMENT TO WEAR RABBEINU TAM'S *TEFILLIN*

The *Aruch haShulchan,* written by Rabbi Yechiel Michel Epstein of Novardok, a definitive work on the Code of Jewish Law, Chapter 34:5, quotes the words of the code regarding Rabbeinu Tam's *tefillin,* "Only someone who is noteworthy in kind and pious acts may wear Rabbeinu Tam's *tefillin,* but the ordinary Jew should not." The *Aruch haShulchan* continues, "Now, since the custom of putting on Rabbeinu Tam's *tefillin* has become a tradition in many communities, there is no issue of 'appearing to be haughty' [by wearing a second pair of *tefillin*], and every person may do so, and may he be blessed for doing so." The Aruch haShulchan was not a *chasid.* However, he lived among *chasidim* and saw for himself how *chasidim* were wearing Rabbeinu Tam's *tefillin* and that they enhanced their service of God. He realized that it did not make one feel haughty; therefore, he recommended and encouraged it, saying that one who wears them, "May he be blessed for doing so."

THE ARIZAL'S AUTHORITATIVE RULING

The Holy Arizal, who is an authority accepted by all Jews, writes (*Pre Etz Chaim, Shaar haTefillin,*

Chapters 9 and 10) that in the time of *Ikvasa d'Meshica,* the "heels" of *Moshiach,* referring to the last moments prior to *Moshiach's* arrival (see the Mishnah, end of Tractate *Sotah,* for clarification), it is an *obligation* to put on Rabbeinu Tam's *tefillin.* The idea of Rabbeinu Tam's *tefillin* being optional is only in regard to whether to put them on simultaneously with the Rashi's *tefillin* or whether to put them on after one has taken off Rashi's *tefillin.* The Arizal's *pesak,* halachic ruling, has been available for over five hundred years.

The Kamarner Rabbi (Atzei Eden of *Mishnah Menachos,* Chapter 4) says that in the times of Rashi and Rabbeinu Tam, those who lived in Rashi's community followed Rashi and those who lived in Rabbeinu Tam's community followed Rabbeinu Tam. However, now, years after their passing, it is obligatory to put on both pairs of *tefillin.* We also find support for this in the *sefer Chayim Shaul* from the great Sephardic authority the *Chida'a,* Rabbi Chaim Yosef Dovid Azulai.

Chasidim have been pioneers in universally implementing this good practice, which today is law, as ruled by the Arizal. Now, let the rest of the Jewish world join together and begin wearing a second pair of *tefillin.*

17

Candle Lighting for Girls

Chasidism has also reminded Traditional Judaism of another custom that has been neglected; the lighting of *Shabbos* and holiday candles by girls of all ages.

TORAH SOURCE

"And Yitzchok brought her [Rivkah] into the tent of his mother Sarah" (*Bereishit* 24:67). On the words, "Into the tent . . . ," Rashi comments: "He brought her into the tent, and behold, she was like Sarah his mother, meaning, she became like Sarah his mother. For as long as Sarah lived, there was a light burning from one *Erev Shabbos* to the next, a blessing was found in the dough, and a cloud hovered over the tent. When she died these ceased; when Rivkah entered the tent, they returned." The verse continues, "And he took Rivkah and she became his wife."

The juxtaposition of these two statements is not coincidental. When Yitzchok saw the aforementioned qualities in Rivkah (one of which was that her candles remained lit for the full week), he realized that her righteousness was equal to that of his mother, Sarah, and consequently he married her. This shows that Rivkah used to light *Shabbos* candles even before she was married. Furthermore, according to Rashi, Rivkah was only three years old when she married Yitzchok. Nevertheless, she already lit *Shabbos* candles, although she was well below the age of obligation to perform *mitzvos*.

ARUCH HASHULCHAN'S VIEW

We find from a number of other sources that until fairly recent generations, it was the widespread custom in many Jewish communities for girls to light candles. To quote the *Aruch haShulchan,* " . . . it is customary for each Jewish girl to light her own candle even when she is in her parents' home . . . for this commandment is mainly relevant to them . . . each one saying a blessing upon the candles. . . ."

The following is a partial list of those rabbinic families whose daughters have verified that it was their custom for even young girls to light candles: Alter (Ger); Halberstam (Tzanz-Bobov); Hager (Vishnitz); Karelitz (Chazon Ish); Rokeach (Belz); Schneerson (Lubavitch); Shapiro (Volozhin); Soloveitchik (Brisk); and Sonenfeld (Jerusalem). The great Gaonim, Rabbis Yosef Ber and Rafael Soloveitchik, said that this was the custom of their parents and grandparents, and so in their own home the girls light *Shabbos* candles. The Bobver *chasidim* say that their custom was taken from Kaminka (another chasidic group), where they would place a candle in the hand of a newborn girl on the first *Erev Shabbos* of her life.

WHY DID THE CUSTOM WANE?

Accordingly, one may ask: If the custom was indeed widespread, why is it not so prevalent today? In answering, one must remember the upheavals and economic difficulties in the first half of this century, and particularly during World War I, which brought, in addition to financial hardships, a well-known shortage of candle wax. It was difficult enough for families to acquire two candles (and sometimes even one candle) for the lady of the house to light. This made it virtually impossible for most families to continue the custom, and the custom waned.

SHABBOS CANDLES: CREATIVE INDEPENDENCE FOR GIRLS

In September 1974, the Lubavitcher Rebbe, Rabbi Menachem Mendel Schneerson, initiated a campaign that every Jewish girl should light a candle of her own and say the blessing. He explained that even though the Torah obligation to light *Shabbos* candles lies upon the mother it is part of the *mitzvah* of *chinuch,* education, to train girls in the practice of *mitzvos* that they will do as they grow up and get married. This custom is for girls both before and after *bas mitzvah.* Parents should not fear that the lighting of a candle by their teenage daughter will diminish her respect for her mother's authority. In our day and age, when attitudes have drastically changed and girls look much further afield in order to develop an independent identity, a girl's active participation in the lighting of candles can help channel this independence in a direction that will strengthen her relationship with her mother, her family, and her heritage.

FROM WHAT AGE SHOULD A GIRL LIGHT?

As soon as a girl is able to speak she should light a candle, even if she is only one year old. In addition to the reinforcement of Jewish values that she receives through lighting candles, there is a light that is brought into the world each time a candle is lit. Since we live in a time when spiritual darkness is pervasive, any additional *mitzvah* or custom (based on *halachah*) is positive and very much needed. *Shabbos* candles bring spiritual light into the world. When a girl of one year lights a candle, she actually draws light into the physical universe. She made it happen!

HOW MANY CANDLES SHOULD A GIRL LIGHT?

The Lubavitcher Rebbe suggested that a single girl should light one candle. This is to differentiate between her and one who is already married, since it is the custom of married women to light at least two candles. It might be interpreted as disrespectful if a girl were to light the same number of candles as her mother.

WHERE SHOULD SHE LIGHT THEM?

The girl should light them in the same place as her mother, on the *Shabbos* table. Each girl should have her own candlestick.

WHO SHOULD LIGHT FIRST?

It is halachically preferable that a girl light before her mother. From a practical point of view as well, a girl should light before her mother, so that her mother may help her light the match or move the candlestick, if necessary. (Once the mother has lit her candles, she has accepted *Shabbos* and must refrain from all labor, including the lighting of matches, the moving of the candlestick, etc.)

The lighting of *Shabbos* candles by girls and women of all ages is a widespread Jewish custom accepted by many Traditional Jewish leaders. Chasidim have reinforced this practice and shown how it instills a Torah-oriented independence in the life of Jewish girls.

18

Niggunim, Chasidic Melodies

Music in Judaism dates back to the earliest of times. In Genesis, the Torah tells us that Yuval was the father of music. King Dovid composed the Book of Psalms using his harp. The Prophets, as the Torah narrates, used music as a means to enter the esoteric realms. Traditional Jews have beautiful music, particularly in the form of *zemiros,* songs, which are sung at the *Shabbos* table. What does chasidic music contribute?

Chasidic teachings and practices introduce us to a new and different approach through the *niggun,* a tune or melody. The *niggun* is the pen of the heart. Jews have two "souls," two basic drives that enliven them. One is animalistic in nature, the other is godly. The godly soul needs nourishment, and one of the foods for the soul is the *niggun.* It is through the *niggun* that the godly soul can acquire the strength to incorporate the animalistic soul and the body into the service of God. Traditional Judaism has always emphasized the proper tune both in learning Talmud and in prayer. Chasidus adds the dimension of the *niggun* as a service to God in and of itself.

HISTORY OF *NIGGUNIM*

Some *niggunim* consist of melodies with words and others don't have any words, only melody. Each *niggun* has a meaning, each *niggun* says something. *Chasidim* would *zog ah niggun,* say a *niggun*, not sing a *niggun*. The reason is that a *niggun* conveys a message that motivates a person to become better. The *niggunim* that have words can only express what the words mean. On the other hand, *niggunim* that have no lyrics are limitless in that one is able to express feelings that cannot be captured by language.

DETAILS OF *NIGGUNIM*

Niggunim were brought to the Jewish community from several different sources, one being the traditional melodies of the local shepherd who spent his days in the open, surrounded by the beautiful hills and mountains. He would lift his eyes towards God and express his feelings in the form of a melody. Somehow, *chasidim* heard this tune and felt a deep sincerity. Perhaps its roots went back to ancient times, and even to the songs of the Levites in the *Bais HaMikdash.* They brought it to the *yeshivah* or the synagogue and began singing it. These *niggunim* were often used to help concentration in *davening.*

Other *niggunim* were composed by *chasidim* or by rebbes themselves, such as the ten *niggunim* attributed to Rabbi Shneur Zalman of Liadi. In more recent times, the Modsitzser Rebbe composed many beautiful *niggunim*. Once, before he was about to be operated upon, he refused anesthesia. Instead, he sang a long and meditative *niggun,* which affected him so deeply that he felt no pain during the operation!

Ordinary *chasidim,* while not aspiring to such total physical transformation, can utilize *niggunim* to give the soul greater power over the body. This increases the power of Torah study to actualize this goal by bringing into play those soul powers, which are even higher than intellect.

Some *niggunim* are lively, *ah lebediker niggun,* and others more calm and meditative, known as *ah devekus niggun.* Regardless of what type of *niggun* it is, there is an advantage to singing a *niggun* slowly, so that one can hear what the *niggun* is saying. If one rushes the singing of the *niggun,* he has no idea what the *niggun* teaches. A cantorial voice isn't needed to sing a *niggun*—anyone who wants his heart to express itself in a deep way can learn and sing *niggunim.*

TRANSFORMATION THROUGH *NIGGUNIM*

During my years at home, my father taught my brothers, sister, and myself various *niggunim.* Usually he taught them on *Shabbos* afternoon after we came home from shul. After we ate, we children wanted to leave the table and run outside to play. He said to us, ''*Shabbos* is a time to relax, not rush your meal, and to sing *niggunim.*'' He made us stay at the table and listen to him sing. He would close his eyes and sing with tremendous devotion. After certain tunes he would express to us his true desire in life, which was to forget about all materialistic pursuits and cleave only to God. He wasn't saintly or angelic; he was simply expressing a Jew's true goal in life, namely communion with God. During the *niggun* he went through a transformation, and we children experienced it too. None of us were superhuman; we were very simple, average people. It was the power of the *niggun* that made the difference in us.

Initially when my father would sing, I was bored. I wanted to leave, but he put his foot down and insisted, "You're staying here until I'm finished." I wasn't happy about that, but nevertheless I listened and listened. Years later, as a teenager in *yeshivah,* I developed a love for *niggunim.* I would fall asleep listening to them. It took many hours to learn each and every part of the *niggun,* but I had the desire and patience to listen to it over and over until I mastered the melody. Here was part of the transformation. Despite my childhood boredom, the impact of the *niggun* took hold and came back to me later in life.

WHY SING AND BE HAPPY?
SHOULDN'T A PERSON BE SERIOUS?

Chasidim are known for their joy and fervor. Some people regard it as shallow and silly. After all, shouldn't man, the epitome of creation, be a serious thinker, a philosopher? How can such a person have time to sing and dance to God, when he should be occupied with higher things? Indeed, *chasidim* are very serious and rational people, but there is something special in their joy.

A great rabbi once said that a person without a feeling for *niggunim* doesn't have a feeling for Chasidus. What should he need to have a feeling for *nig-*

gunim? Of course, this feeling for *niggunim* does not mean being a talented musician. Rather, it means an appreciation for something special the *niggun* brings into one's life. *Niggunim* were created or adopted by great and saintly individuals who were expressing their yearning for God and their cleaving to God. These songs have the power to move others in that same direction. Thus, a feeling for *niggunim* is a movement in oneself toward God, a desire to cleave to God, ultimately to be absorbed in God.

Rabbi Yosef Yitzchok Schneerson explains the reason that a *niggun* has this potential: "The reason that singing can set up such a connection is that melody is made up of movements, and all movement gives rise to warmth, which is a vessel for vitality." Movement creates energy and warmth. A stone has no fire or warmth, but when it rubs against another stone, sparks will come forth; so it is for a *niggun* with its movements. When we sing these movements it stimulates our spiritual energy and results in a warmth which can connect us to the spiritual energy of those who created the *niggunim* in their yearnings and movements toward God.

REPETITION OF MELODY

Another feature of the *niggun* is that it is sung over and over. One may sing it many times; indeed, *chasidim* often will sing the same *niggun* for hours. The purpose certainly is not to learn it well—this could happen with a few repetitions. The truth is that they are like the person who is so taken by a work of art that he gazes at it for hours. It is not just a matter of admiring the talent of the artist in drawing, color, or proportion, but of being drawn into it, becoming absorbed by it. If another person walks by and asks, "What are you looking at?" there is really no answer. There is no "you" who is looking. Likewise, singing the *niggun* enables one literally to lose oneself and become absorbed in God. So *niggunim* are sung by those yearning, seeking, and ultimately uniting with God.

This is why a *niggun* is similar to Chasidus, and a person without an appreciation for *niggunim* cannot appreciate Chasidus. The purpose of both is to become absorbed in God. With the *niggun,* knowing the melody is a step, but only one step on the path. Likewise, studying Chasidus is important—we must understand God, ourselves, and the universe through metaphors, parables, and morals from everyday life. However, the purpose of the study is not merely to gain information. The accomplishment of Chasidus is to be absorbed in the unknown. Study is to be accompanied by active meditation, a search for the true meaning of what is learned. When the student internalizes what he learns, when it is with him during prayer, then a different experience comes about. The material learned becomes an entryway into deep thought that activates other levels and ultimately brings the person to another level of experience. We can call this level total transformation.

The basic striving of a Jew is to be absorbed within God, the desire to be lost and absorbed in the higher power that is beyond our understanding; and this is what chasidic *niggunim* help us attain. *Zemiros,* traditional *Shabbos* songs, have greatness, however they were composed with a specific theme and lesson in mind, therefore they are limited. Chasidic *niggunim,* with their movement beyond limitations, have something to contribute to all Jews.

19

Studying Chasidus

Among the basic tenets of the chasidic movement is the studying of chasidic teachings. Chasidus, as set forth by the Baal Shem Tov, is the study of divinity, and the leaders of Chasidus, in particular Chabad Chasidus, have developed a Torah system of thought which communicates the profound oneness of God in a way that can be appreciated and utilized by mankind.

Kabbalah is called "the soul of Torah," but it is only accessible to those with lofty souls. Chasidus uses metaphors and analogies to make its ideas accessible for the average person. Its power to bring godliness to all has earned it the title of the "soul of the soul" of Torah. The result is an intimacy with God that formerly belonged to the select few. The practical consequences are a deepened faith in and love of God, which translates into greater enthusiasm for divine service.

This branch of Torah study necessitates regular learning and focused concentration. For this reason,

Rabbi Sholom Dovber Schneerson established the *Yeshivah Tomchei Tmimim,* where students could apply themselves to Chasidus with the same energy and enthusiasm they give to Talmud. He said, "There are plenty of *yeshivos* throughout Europe in which they study Talmud. However, there isn't one *yeshivah* where they study Chasidus for several hours daily, the same way, analyzing each word and asking difficult and detailed questions." Another goal was to put focus on *davening.* The learning of Chasidus was a preparation for *davening* with *chayus,* zest and warmth. *Davening* was not something incidental. It came between the learning of Chasidus and the learning of Talmud and was as important as either.

The idea of learning Chasidus in the same way as Talmud was not institutionalized prior to the advent of Chasidus. Traditional Jews, beginning from the Vilna Gaon's days until today, did not emphasize the learning of *Mussar* as the *chasidim* did with Chasidus. This was the case in the most *Mussar*-oriented *yeshivos.* Again, the reason was the imperative for the students to put the vast majority of their time, energy, and interest into the study of the Talmud. Even among the other chasidic groups, there wasn't an emphasis on learning Chasidus daily and with the same devotion as Talmud.

The Chabad-Lubavitcher *chasidim* have taken the words of *Moshiach* literally. When the Baal Shem Tov asked *Moshiach* when he was coming, he said, "When the wellsprings of Chasidus will disseminate to the furthest corners on earth." (This question and answer is printed in a book of collected letters of the Baal Shem Tov and his students, *Lwow* 5683, wherein the publisher writes that he copied this letter from the one handwritten by the Baal Shem Tov's son-in-law, Reb

Yechiel, which was signed personally by the Baal Shem Tov. This letter is also printed in the book *Ginzei Nistaros* [Jerusalem, 5684], I, Chapter 65. A portion of the letter is also printed at the beginning of *Keser Shem Tov,* section 1 [p. 2a–b].) This means that one must study Chasidus every day and with clear understanding. Compared to the essence of the soul, human intellect is a "far corner." Chasidus also demands that this study influence the emotions, which are yet further removed from the core of one's being. In turn, such conscientious study confers the ability to communicate properly the essence of Chasidus, the soul of Torah, to those who may temporarily be on the outside. This will cause them to take a peek in, and eventually approach the inner chambers of God.

DO NOT WITHHOLD INFORMATION

When the previous Lubavitcher Rebbe came to America he said, "I do not have a copyright on disseminating Torah and *mitzvos.*" The same is true with the serious studying of Chasidus. Chabad's emphasis on learning Chasidus isn't for *chabadniks* only, but rather for all Jews. As the Alter Rebbe said, "I don't want to make Chabad Chasidism a party" (as for example, the Republican Party), rather it is for all Jews. On the contrary, if the *chabadnik* doesn't share the beauty and importance of studying Chasidus on a daily basis with all Jews, but keeps it for himself, it is considered a very selfish thing and not at all in the spirit of the *Moshiach's* response to the Baal Shem Tov.

Rabbi Shneur Zalman, the Alter Rebbe, in his introduction to the *Tanya,* says that those *chasidim* who are not able to find counsel from the *Tanya* should approach the older *chasidim* who will explain to them and show them how the *Tanya* does indeed address their issues. The Alter Rebbe says, ''Great is the punishment for those who hoard grain and great is the reward,'' (for giving of their time to those who are less knowledgeable, not just academically, but in knowledge of their spiritual path). Let all Jews benefit from the wellsprings of Chasidus.

WHAT DID THE VILNA GAON SAY ABOUT LEARNING THE ESOTERIC WISDOM OF TORAH?

The following material has been compiled from Rabbi J. Immanuel Schochet's book *The Mystical Dimension* (vol. 1).

1. Rabbi Chaim of Voloszin quotes his master, Rabbi Eliyahu of Vilna, known as the Gaon, to the effect that it is absolutely impossible to speak of a contradiction between the Talmud and *Zohar,* between the exoteric (revealed) and the esoteric (mystical) facets of the Torah. (See quotations and references cited in B. Landau, *Hagaon Hachasid MeVilna* [Jerusalem, 1967], pp. 140–141).

2. In *Even Shlomo* (VIII:21), the Vilna Gaon is quoted as stating that knowledge of *sod,* Jewish mysticism, is essential for a clear understanding of *peshat,* the simple textual meaning.

3. The Vilna Gaon comments on Midrash *Mishlei,* Chapter 10, that the obligation to study *Pnimiyus haTorah* applies even to the wicked whose conduct is far removed from the Torah way of life (*Even Shlomo* 8:24 and note 20 there).

4. In *Even Shlomo* (VIII:27) the Vilna Gaon is quoted as saying that it is specifically the preoccupation with *Pnimiyus haTorah* that offers protection against the *yetzer hara.* (See also his comment on *Yeshayahu* 6:10 in *Kol Eliyahu,* p. 60f.)

5. The Vilna Gaon is quoted in *Even Shlomo* (XI:7) as applying the Torah command "Guard My charge" (the obligation to take precautionary measures for the preservation and guarding of the divine instructions of the Torah) to suggest the studying of *Pnimiyus haTorah* as a way to battle the spiritual deterioration of the generations in *galus,* exile.

20

Farbrengen

A *farbrengen* is an informal gathering in which people get together to celebrate their Judaism by means of song, stories, and words of inspiration. Some *chasidim* call this activity a *tish,* literally meaning a table, referring to the chasidic custom of going to one's rebbe's table to hear words of Torah. Traditional Jews will also increase their learning of Torah and doing of *mitzvos* by incorporating the *farbrengen* into their life-style.

SINGING OF *NIGGUNIM* AT A *FARBRENGEN*

What happens at a *farbrengen?* Chasidic melodies which have no words, called *niggunim,* are sung. Meditative and inspirational in nature, they often bring the singer and listener to the verge of tears, and many people have testified that hearing these melodies was their first step toward a true return to God. The wordlessness of the songs suggests the openness of the meeting, going beyond the limitations of language.

SAYING *L'CHAIM*

Traditionally, some alcoholic drink is also shared, for it is understood that a small amount of alcohol can be a heart opener, for the mind often limits the expression of our heart. We hold back our true emotions because our intellect builds defenses, saying to us, "Everything is just fine the way it us; you don't need to change." When we toast *"L'chaim!"* we loosen our corporeality and begin to open ourselves to the truth by sharing with others what's in our hearts and minds.

HEARING STORIES OF *TZADDIKIM*

The leader usually tells stories of great *tzaddikim* of the past, or the heroic figures he has known in his own life. In the *yeshivah,* where I attended many *farbrengens,* the stories came alive because one could see the character transformation that had happened to the person who told the story. Here was a living being who practiced what he preached, who had internalized what he had learned, and expected the same of others.

After a few short stories, the leader encourages others to open up and, in simple English, "get into it." In response, people support each other to explore their inner selves, to acknowledge their difficulties, and to struggle toward inner truth. This way of opening oneself is healthy and thoroughly rooted in the chasidic way of life. It is not just for *chasidim* with long white beards who sit in *yeshivah* day and night, but for every

Jew—even the younger generation—regardless of age, belief, or level of understanding and observance of Torah. We have to take advantage of such opportunities because we now have the responsibility to carry on the teachings of our heritage.

BEING A PARTICIPANT AT A *FARBRENGEN*

During my years in *yeshivah,* I had many opportunities to participate in these *farbrengens.* I use the word *participate* rather than *attend* to make a point. If we go to a therapist's office, do we listen to the therapist and then sit back and say to ourselves, "That's a wonderful idea—I'll consider it"? If we did, we would be wasting our money. If we want to change (and otherwise why would we be there?) we have to participate, speak up, open ourselves up to the therapist. The same is true for the "group therapy" of a *farbrengen.* To be available for change, a person must decide not to be a bystander but rather a participant.

I recall some of the deep emotions I felt. I wanted simply to let go of my ego and my pride, desiring only to be absorbed within God. For a short moment, the inspiration of the *niggun* was so powerful that there was no "I" who wanted to be one with God. There was only God, who wanted us to be involved in His divine plan. I felt this connection physically, being together with other participants, being like brothers without any jealousy or greed.

THE EMOTIONAL CLEANSING

Sometimes the feelings aroused at a *farbrengen* can be startling. I remember a *farbrengen* with a *chasid* named Reb Mendel, my wife's great-uncle. Reb Mendel's message is that every person must be simple. Any form of ego or conceit has no place in Reb Mendel's world. He communicated this to me very sharply one *Shabbos*. My family and he were sharing the *Shabbos* meal when, as often happened, some of the *yeshivah* students from the neighborhood dropped by. Immediately a *farbrengen* started, with enthusiastic singing. In the middle of the songs, Reb Mendel stopped and told the following story.

Once a *chasid* came to visit the Rebbe. The Rebbe told him to fast for three days, then walk to shul and go up on the *bimah,* the raised platform used for the Torah reading. He was to say to all of the congregation that sending their children to the local Russian schools was forbidden, because the children were being indoctrinated with heresy. The Rebbe added that he should not speak to anyone after making this announcement.

There were many KGB informers in the shul, but the *chasid* had no fear and did what his Rebbe instructed. Years later, Reb Mendel explained, he met this *chasid* at the time everyone was fleeing from Stalin. He related that when the *chasid* recited the prayer before retiring at night, unusual sounds would come from his nose. When he first heard this, Reb Mendel asked the *chasid* if everything was all right. The man responded that, healthwise, everything was fine. However, the courageous act he had done years before in the synagogue, making the announcement in front of informers, had made him feel self-important. His ego had become inflated. Therefore, he was reflecting on this at night before going to sleep. The sounds were his expression of true regret and a call to God to forgive him for the fact that there was a "bad odor" coming from his good deed.

Reb Mendel, as he finished the story, lifted his head, looked out from his overpowering eyebrows, and said, "Dalfin, did you get what we are saying?" I walked away thinking very seriously about my own ego in connection with my good deeds. Even though he had made his point in public, I wasn't insulted because we were all participants. It was a tremendously cleansing experience.

THE *FARBRENGEN* IS FOR OLD AND YOUNG

You can probably find such a *farbrengen* or *tish* in your community, or one nearby, where you can become a regular participant. Adults and students are the usual participants, but parents should take their young children along, too. My wife remembers sitting on her father's lap, listening to the older *chasidim* recalling their days in Russia. She was only five years old when she heard one *chasid* speak to another about a particular character trait, but she remembers it left an indelible impression on her to the present day.

A person must go to a *farbrengen* and become a participant in order to understand it. It does not take long to feel a part of the mood and to overcome one's initial embarrassment. You will come to look forward to sharing with other *chasidim,* for you will discover that they are the ones who truly care for you.

21

The Rebbe Figure

Probably the most significant distinction between Traditional and chasidic Judaism is the idea of having a rebbe. To understand this, we need to take a look at three titles used to describe Jewish leadership.

RABBI, RAV—A TEACHER

The rabbi or rav is a person who has received ordination in a specific area of Jewish Law, for instance, marriage and divorce or the kosher laws. He might be learned in all areas of Jewish Law but unable to give an oration from a pulpit. Sometimes he might be a great speaker but lack the communication skills needed to deal with individuals. Regardless of the particular talents that each rabbi has, they all have one thing in common: they communicate Jewish Law. The Torah has advice for all issues, but the rabbi must tell the person who is seeking advice to such questions as, "What is my

mission in life?'' or ''Where should I live to fulfill my
mission?'' that to these questions he has no answers
because they are not part of his job!

A REBBE—A SPIRITUAL GUIDE

The second title is Rebbe. A rebbe is someone who addresses the needs of people's souls. Questions involving
one's spiritual direction are the main reason for going to a
rebbe. The Mishnah, in Ethics of the Fathers (2:1), says,
''Rebbe says, which path should a person choose?'' From
a *chasidic* perspective, the inner meaning of the Mishnah
can be understood by looking carefully at the words. It is
the responsibility of a rebbe to show a person which path
he should choose. Notice the Mishnah does not say, ''Rav
says,'' because it is not the job of a rav to deal with issues
that involve what path one should choose.

Since a rebbe's purpose is to give spiritual direction,
he need not necessarily function as a rav, in the sense of
giving halachic rulings. This difference is illustrated by
the following story about the Kotzker Rebbe: A *chasid*
once came to have a private audience. The Kotzker Rebbe asked him why he came. He responded that he came
for guidance on how to find God. The Rebbe said, ''To
find God you do not need to come to a rebbe; one can
find God in the Torah, that is, the *halachah,* by going to a
rav. The reason one comes to a rebbe is to find oneself!''

EVERY CHASIDIC GROUP HAS A REBBE,
JUST AS THE TWELVE TRIBES EACH HAD A LEADER

In the chasidic world, the word *rebbe* denotes a leader
of a chasidic group. He provides guidance in day-to-day

issues. The *chasidim* believe that their rebbe is their link to God. This means that regardless of the fact that every *chasid* has a connection to God, it is the rebbe who tells them how to actualize that connection. Since human beings are shortsighted in their vision and perception, one goes to the rebbe, who has been granted insight.

Just as in the times of Moshe Rabbeinu, the Jewish people were composed of twelve tribes, each with its leader, so it is with the chasidic world, each chasidic group having its rebbe. There are many rebbes, each with *chasidim*. Each chasidic group follows a certain version of the Baal Shem Tov's teachings. This is so because the entire notion of *chasid* and rebbe as defined here was started by the Baal Shem Tov and his disciples. Since he had many students, each practiced and emphasized a different aspect of his teachings. Because of this, today there are some *chasidim* who shout their prayers, while others say them quietly. These differences and hundreds of others are a direct result of practices associated with the students of the Baal Shem Tov.

One aspect of the rebbe–*chasid* relationship is the *yechidus* experience, a private audience between *chasid* and rebbe, during which they form a strong bond with each other. The *chasid* will usually ask the rebbe for guidance in both spiritual and material matters. Another is through attending the rebbe's *tish,* meaning the *Shabbos* and holiday table, where the *chasid* joins the rebbe at his festive meal. At his rebbe's table he sees how the rebbe acts and speaks, and he listens to Torah interpretations that lift him above the mundane. He participates in the chasidic melodies sung by the rebbe and the *chasidim*. In Chabad circles this takes the form of a *farbrengen,* an informal gathering with the rebbe at its center.

SHIRAYIM, THE LEFTOVERS OF FOOD AND DRINK

Finally, the *chasid* eats some of the leftover food from the rebbe's plate, known as *shirayim.* This practice is supported by two principles taught in the Talmud. "He who partakes of a meal at which a sage is present, it is as if he feasted on the splendor of the *Shechinah*" (*Berachos* 64a), and in the Jerusalem Talmud (*Moed Katan* 2:3) we find that Rabbi Yochanan gathered and consumed the crumbs remaining from a *se'udat mitzvah,* a meal connected with a *mitzvah,* and said, "May I be counted among those who partook in that meal."

The drinking of wine over which the rebbe has made a blessing is especially powerful, since the wine of *kos shel berachah,* the cup over which one recites the grace after meals, and by extension, other blessings, is itself a source of blessing (*Berachos* 51:b)

A REBBE WHO IS THE MOSHE RABBEINU OF THE GENERATION, THE *NASI,* THE LEADER

Unique among all the rebbes is a very special type of which there is only one in a generation. This rebbe is not just a leader for his own *chasidim,* he is a rebbe for all the Jewish people of his generation. We call him a Rebbe, a *Nasi.* Moshe Rabbeinu was an example of such a rebbe. Moshe himself, speaking to God about appointing a future leader after his passing, describes the leader in the following way: "Let the Omnipotent God of all living souls appoint a man over the community. Let him come and go before them, and let him bring forth and lead them. Let God's community not be like sheep that have no shepherd." (*Pinchos* 27:16) It is understood that Moshe himself was such an individual and therefore desired someone with the same qualities to replace him.

The Midrash (*Bereishis Rabbah* 56:7) says that in every generation there is a leader like Moshe. The *Tikunei Zohar* (69:114a) says that there is an extension of Moshe in every generation. There can only be one of this type. As the Talmud says (*Sanhedrin* 18a), there is only one leader for each generation, not two leaders. Rashi comments (*Chukas* 21:21) that the leader of the generation is like the entire generation. True, there are leaders of groups, just as there were leaders for each tribe. However, just as there was one Moshe and one Yehoshua, so too there is only one rebbe who is the Rebbe, the *Nasi,* of all Jews.

REBBE IS AN ACRONYM FOR *ROSH BNEI YISROEL*

The Hebrew letters that make up the word *rebbe* are an acronym for *Rosh Bnei Yisroel,* the head of the people of Israel. Just as the head, the seat of the brain and the faculties of sight, smell, hearing, and speech, actually controls the body, so too the rebbe heads and controls the Jewish people who are compared to the body. Being the head, he cannot be defined as someone who excels only in Torah knowledge or in the practice of *mitzvos.* Nor is he merely a miracle maker or charismatic figure.

To summarize, a rebbe activates miracles, he knows the entire Torah, he gives advice, but these are what he does, not what he is. A rebbe is a rebbe, and because he is a rebbe he not only has every form of human perfection but he also goes beyond the limitations of humanity as much as is possible for a creature of flesh and blood.

REBBE FOR ALL

A rebbe in the fullest sense isn't just a rebbe for his followers and admirers but for all Jews. He is the living symbol of God's energy in the universe. He reveals God's essence and qualities more than anyone else because his entire being is an expression of Godliness. In general, all human and even angelic beings have their own independent will, and only after an internal process of commitment do they submit their will to God. However, a rebbe has been granted a soul that has the power to completely submit to God and emulate His ways. Granted that every single Jew has a part of God in his godly soul, the *neshomah,* but he tends to forget its essence and allow the world and its temptations, whether physical or even spiritual, to take control. A rebbe's *neshomah* comes from a higher place. It not only stands higher than the other *neshomah* and in a sense includes them, but it is immune to the darkness of this world. It thus enables him to help each individual along the path of life. As *chasidim* would say, *"ah rebbe iz ah geborena zach nisht ah gevorana zach,"* he is born, not made.

REBBE HAS *CHASIDIM*

Just as *chasidim* need a rebbe, so does a rebbe need *chasidim.* Chasidus uses the idea of a king as a parable. For a king to be a king he needs subjects. If they do not feel like being subjects, then there is no one to carry out his orders, and thus he fails to be a king. He could have a palace, a throne, and plenty of treasures, but with no one to accept his leadership, he is just another celebrity. The same is the case with *chasidim.* There are no *chasidim* without a rebbe, but there is also no rebbe without *chasidim.*

For the *chasid,* the rebbe is his whole life and he will give his life, literally, for his rebbe. To him, the rebbe is a living Torah. Just as if a *sefer Torah* were, God forbid, about to be burned in a fire, one would jump into the fire, jeopardizing his life, so too with the ''living Torah,'' the rebbe.

REBBE INFORMS US WHAT WE NEED TO DO

When a rebbe gives direction to an individual or to a group of people, he is informing them of God's desire at that time and place. *Chasidim* believe that when a rebbe tells someone to move from California to Costa Rica, it isn't necessarily because the rebbe knows the person will succeed financially in Costa Rica, but rather that the rebbe, being permeated by Torah, communicates to the person what Torah says is best for him.

YECHIDUS, PRIVATE AUDIENCE WITH THE REBBE

This information comes from the very essence of the rebbe, his superconscious, and connects with the person's essence. This is known as the *yechidus* experience, meaning oneness. At that time, the rebbe's essence unites and becomes one with the person's essence. The rebbe does not have to know the person; he might never have known him prior to his *yechidus* encounter. However, this makes absolutely no difference because all Jews are one essence, as it is written, "We all have one father."

This essential relationship between the Jew and the rebbe has been tested in many different ways and has proven to be successful. For example, people from all over the world have come to see Rabbi M. M. Schneerson, the Lubavitcher Rebbe. The Rebbe instructed them to do some particular thing, and they followed his advice. Some found solutions to their problems, others became transformed through a commitment to Torah and *mitzvos,* and yet others became *chasidim.* This is because the Torah has all the answers for everyone, everywhere. It is all a matter of finding them. A rebbe helps the individual and the community to find the God-given guidance for their lives. A rebbe is not a stargazer; a rebbe is a pointer. He points to that part of Torah that is just right. It may take the form of telling people where to live, what to eat, or what sort of occupation to pursue, or he may give advice on specific *mitzvos,* Jewish customs, or Torah studies.

EACH PERSON HAS A LETTER IN TORAH THAT CONNECTS HIM OR HER TO GOD

The Torah itself says every person has a letter in the Torah, meaning there is a specific letter in the Torah that is one's personal guide. The Hebrew word *Yisroel* is an acronym for several other Hebrew words, these being: "There are six hundred thousand letters in the Torah." Just as there are six hundred thousand "general souls," each soul incorporating other souls, thus including all Jewish souls, so too the Torah has six hundred thousand letters that incorporate all Jews, giving everyone a direct link to Torah. There is a story concerning the Ramban and his student, Avnr, which illustrates the point that everyone has a letter in Torah.

Avnr left his teacher and became a heretic. He came to the Ramban and told him that the reason he did so was that he was told that every person's name can be found in the Torah portion of *Haazinu* in the book of *Devarim,* and he had looked and could not find his name. Therefore he felt that everything he had learned was not true, and he left Judaism. The Ramban told him to look into the portion of *Haazinu* 32:26 where the verse reads," . . . *afaihem asveso menush zcrom."* The third letter in each of these four Hebrew words spells the name *Avnr.* Avnr was amazed, and he left and traveled far away to do *teshuvah* for his heresy. We see from this story that not only does everyone have a letter in Torah, but one also has his name in the Torah. However, since most people are nowhere near refined enough to see it, God wants them to meet with a rebbe to help them find their own letter in the Torah.

The Book of Proverbs says that "a *mitzvah* is a candle, and the Torah is light." When a rebbe announces that the world needs an increase in the study of Talmud and Chasidus, or that all Jews should increase their giving of charity, he is actually saying that this will bring an additional light of Godliness into the world, and in turn eliminate the darkness. When a rebbe calls for all Jewish children to have a letter written for them in a Torah scroll, he is telling us that this is the call of the hour. He sees something we do not. He is refined in his character and behavior, so he is able to see what we do not. The rebbe sees the truth, and he sees it from God's perspective, not the human perspective. As the Talmud quotes Psalms 25:14, "God shares his secret with those who fear Him."

THE CONCEPT OF A REBBE IS NOT NEW

The Jewish people's first rebbe was Moshe Rabbeinu. Moshe instructed them on what to do and did so in the name of God. Eventually Moshe was advised by Yisro to deal only with the "big" matters, and leave everything else to his appointees in order to concentrate on his main responsibility, leading the Jewish people.

A rebbe is in the same position. One cannot visit with the rebbe at all times; if one has something that needs attention, he turns to the elder *chasidim* for guidance. If they in turn do not have the answers, one writes a letter to the rebbe, and if there is still no reply, only then does one arrange for a private audience with the rebbe. King Dovid was the rebbe in his times and King Shlomo was the rebbe in his times, and so in every generation there is a rebbe who is the *Nasi*.

DIFFERENT REBBES; CHOOSING A REBBE FOR YOURSELF

Among the different chasidic groups there are many rebbes. How does one know which rebbe is for him? Some may go around shopping until a certain rebbe fits their style. This approach has little chance of releasing them from ego and bringing them close to God, since they are looking for a rebbe who will fit their needs.

Others, however, are absorbed and lose themselves in the rebbe. Their soul connects with a certain rebbe in a way that transcends words. It just happens. It could be compared to meeting one's soul mate. Some find a chain of reasons why they should be together. Others say it is "chemistry," but it is really the call of one soul to another.

This is the most refined and spiritual way of identifying with a rebbe. When one lets go of his ego and surrenders to the rebbe, one knows and feels it is right in every way. As far as The Rebbe The *Nasi* is concerned, there are no choices; there is only one per generation who is appointed by God as the leader and head of all Jews, whether they understand and agree or not. It is irrelevant, just as the Jews had no option as to whether or not they wanted Moshe as their rebbe, as we see from the story of *Korach* (Numbers 16). So too, the Jews do not have a choice as to who is The Rebbe The *Nasi*; he has been appointed by God.

TRADITIONAL JEWS AND A REBBE

Many Traditional Jews, beginning from the Vilna Gaon's times, have for the most part not accepted the idea of a rebbe. However, as time goes on and we come closer to the arrival of *Moshiach,* they have begun looking into this idea, coming to the realization that the concept of a rebbe is as old as the Torah itself. Let all Jews unite and realize that having a rebbe is good and needed for themselves and their families.

Epilogue

At this point it is my hope that you, the reader, have taken the time necessary to reflect on the basic ideas of this book, which are threefold: first, that Chasidism has contributed an integral part to our Torah; second, that this contribution has its roots in the Torah; third, that Traditional Judaism has adopted some, and is in the process of adopting more, chasidic ideas and practices.

I want to conclude with several basic chasidic practices that one can test oneself with, to see where one is at and where one is going. This checklist is not the only way for one to be a practicing *chasid,* and at the same time, the fulfillment of these points does not automatically mean that one is a *chasid.* Rather, these are general day-to-day issues that the *chasid* is faced with. Therefore, I mention these points, not to the exclusion of any others. They are not in any particular order; to find out which are most relevant to oneself, it is necessary to consult a *mashpia,* a spiritual-chasidic guide.

THE SUGGESTED CHECKLIST OF A CHASID

1. True *ahavas Yisroel,* fulfilling the chasidic adage "My piece of bread is yours as it is mine," always thinking about the other person first, before thinking about oneself.
2. Learning Chasidus regularly and talking about it with friends and family.
3. Connecting to the rebbe, seeking his guidance on all issues of life.
4. Serving God with *simchah* and enthusiasm.
5. Immersing oneself in the *mikvah* on a regular basis. (Men)
6. Girls of all ages should light *Shabbos* candles. (Women)
7. Putting on Rabbeinu Tam's *tefillin* and wearing a *gartel.* (Men)
8. Eating and drinking only *cholov Yisroel* products.
9. *Davening* with focused concentration without consulting the clock.
10. Engaging in *iskafya,* not indulging in pleasures just because they are permitted.
11. Growing a full untrimmed beard. (Men)
12. Participating in *farbrengens.*

These points are not only intended for the existing *chasid* as a checklist but also for all those Traditional Jews who do not want to be chasidic and/or do not know enough about chasidic practices and customs to make an informed decision. It is for all these people that I have written this book. My hope is to expose them to an approach to God that enhances their already existing life-style.

In very simple words, I am not out to make you, the reader, a *chasid*. I want you to be who you are. However, I trust that your sincerity in finding new ways to enhance your service to God will open your mind to exploring the ideas presented. When you do this, you will see how chasidic practices and customs are for you and all others who are not necessarily chasidic.

As for the argument from *mesorah,* my family tradition, as to how one can deviate from a long line and tradition of not being a *chasid?* First of all, do not be sure that your ancestors were not *chasidim;* a hundred years or more of "enlightenment" in Europe and America have confused the question of origins. Second of all, some leaders of Traditional Judaism came from chasidic families. Third, there were great Torah scholars who became chasidic and broke the family tradition, such as Rabbi Akiva Eiger's grandson, Reb Shlomo Eiger, one of Rabbi Yecheskel Laundau's (the *Noda B'yihuda*) sons, Reb Yankel, the Baal Shem Tov's brother-in-law, Reb Gershon Kitover, who originally was an ardent opponent of Chasidus and his own brother-in-law. The list goes on. If it is all right for these Torah giants, it is all right for you!

The halachic justification for the change of one's *mesorah,* tradition, can be found in *Sedei Chemed* (*kllolim, erech minhag,* pp. 453a–453b), "In each generation there are new rabbinic enactments, and all are the word of God. In the name of the Divrei Yosef, he writes that one can change the *minhag,* custom, peacefully and properly, and there is no concern that one is forsaking 'the Torah of his parents,' since we find that the Baalei Tosfes, the Rosh, and other great rabbis changed many of their *minhagim.*"

Rabbi Zalman Sorotzkin, in his *sefer Moznayim Limishpot,* Chapter 61, addresses this issue in regard to the setting up of formal, organized schools for girls. He says (in reponse to those that opposed this since it was not the custom of our parents to do this):

> Tell the people who have this concern that our generation is not like the earlier generations. They were like angels and upright, enlightened men who lived in a time and environment that did not have to contend with the outside negative forces creeping in to the most religious homes. However, in our generation, when we are men of darkness, and many have lost their faith in God, it is improper not to educate our girls. Anyone who does not attend a school of Torah, man or woman, is severing themselves from life.

In the event that one can trace his ancestry to the time before the Baal Shem Tov, and still not find any *chasidim,* the response is simple. First, one can remain a Traditional Jew while incorporating more Torah practices, encouraged by Chasidism, into his or her tradition. Second, maybe it is time to take another look to see if some things that were always done by all Jews have simply dropped out of your tradition for no good reason. Third, maybe you do not actually have a tradition. If your family has not been practicing Judaism over the last several decades, you, the returnee to Judaism, do not have a set tradition. In such an instance, Torah says, you should join a tradition. Give Chasidus a chance. You will like it.

Glossary

Ahavas Yisroel   loving one's fellow Jew

Akiva   one of the foremost sages of the talmudic period, unlearned until the age of 40, whose ardent efforts enabled him to serve as a major figure in the transmission of the Torah tradition

Alter Rebbe   (lit., "the Old Rebbe") Rabbi Shneur Zalman of Liadi (1745–1812), the founder of the Chabad-Lubavitch trend within the chasidic movement; author of the *Tanya,* a classic text of the chasidic tradition, and *Shulchan Aruch HaRav,* a classic legal code

Amidah   (lit., "standing service"; also known as the silent prayer) the central prayer of the prayer service; also called the *shemoneh esreh*—the Eighteen [blessings]

Avodah (lit., "service") formerly the sacrificial service in the Temple; later, the service of prayer instituted in its stead

Arizal (lit., "the lion of blessed memory") acronym for R. Isaac Luria (1534–1572), one of the leading luminaries of the Kabbalah

Baal Shem Tov (lit., "Master of the Good Name") Rabbi Yisrael ben Eliezer (1698–1760), founder of the chasidic movement

Bais HaMikdash the (First or Second) Temple in Jerusalem

Chabad (acronym for the Hebrew words meaning wisdom, understanding, and knowledge) the approach to Chasidism that filters its spiritual and emotional power through the intellect; a synonym for Chabad is Lubavitch, the name of the town where this movement originally flourished

Chasid (pl. *Chasidim*) a pious person; specifically, the term is used to refer to a follower of a chasidic holy man (rebbe, *tzaddik*) and a member of the chasidic movement of the Baal Shem Tov

Chasidus, Chasidism chasidic thought

Chazon cantor

Cheder (pl. *chadarim*) school in which young children learn reading skills and begin the study of Torah

Chinuch dedication or education

Chutzpah impudence, brazenness

Daven (v) to pray; *davening* (n) Jewish prayer

Devekus   cleaving to God

Emunah   faith

Erev   eve. Generally used for the daylight hours before a holy day, for example, *Erev Shabbos*

Esrog   citron (a particular citrus fruit used during the festival of Succos)

Gaon   a title denoting exceptional rabbinic learning and genius

Gartel   a twined silk belt worn by men during prayer

Halachah   (pl. *halachos*) (a) the body of Torah law; (b) a particular law

Hashem   (lit., "The Name", the four-letter Name of God that cannot be uttered) a way of referring to God

Kabbalah   (lit., "received tradition") the Jewish mystical tradition

Kabbalas ol   (lit., "the acceptance of God's yoke") an unwavering, selfless commitment to carrying out the will of God

Kaddish   a prayer said during the synagogue prayer service. There are a number of forms, the most well known being the one recited as a memorial for the dead

Kavanah   the intention directed toward God while performing a religious deed. Can also mean a particular intention (for a prayer); the plural in that usage is *kavanos*

Kedushah   a responsive prayer said during the synagogue service, when the prayer leader repeats the *Amidah*

Likkutei Dibburim   a selection of the public talks of the sixth Lubavitcher Rebbe, Rabbi Yosef Yitzchok Schneerson

Lulav   a palm branch used for Succos

Maamar   a formal chasidic discourse

Mesiras Nefesh   (lit., "sacrifice of the soul") the willingness to sacrifice oneself, either through martyrdom or through a selfless life, for the sake of the Torah and its commandments

Midrash   classical collection of the sages' homiletic teachings on the Torah

Mikvah   a ritual bath used by women for purification after emerging from the state of *niddah* (spiritual impurity) and used by both men and women in their endeavors to attain spiritual self-refinement

Minchah   the daily afternoon prayer service

Minyan   the minimum prayer quorum of ten

Mishnah   ancient collection of legal decisions of the sages; the earliest part of the Talmud, it is the text to which the Talmud is the commentary

Misnagid   (pl. *Misnagdim*) an opponent of the chasidic movement of the Baal Shem Tov

Moshe Rabbeinu   (lit., "Moses our teacher") the "father of the prophets," who redeemed the Jews from Egypt and brought them to the revelation at Mount Sinai.

Moshiach   (lit., "the anointed one") the Messiah

Mussar   chastisement; ethical teachings

Parshas   the Torah portion of a certain *Shabbos* or festive occasion

Previous Rebbe   Rabbi Yosef Yitzchok Schneerson (1880–1950)

Rabbeinu Tam's Tefillin   tefillin with the four Torah portions arranged in the order prescribed by Rabbi Tam (1100–1171)

Rambam   (acronym for Rabbi Moshe ben Maimon; 1135–1204) Maimonides, one of the foremost Jewish thinkers of the Middle Ages; wrote the *Mishneh Torah, Guide for the Perplexed,* etc.

Rashi   (acronym for Rabbi Shlomo Yitzchaki [1040–1105]) the author of the foremost commentary to the Torah and the Talmud

Reb   a Title of respect; mister

Rebbe   (lit., "my teacher [or master]") saintly Torah leader who serves as spiritual guide to a following of *chasidim*

Rosh Yeshivah   Dean of a *yeshivah* (lit., "sitting"), referring to an academy of Torah studies in which one of the principal methods of learning is dialogue between students to discover the meaning of the teachers' lectures and the underlying texts

Shabbos   the Sabbath

Shechinah   the Divine Presence

Shlomo   King Dovid's son and successor, who built the First Temple in the tenth century

Shulchan Aruch   the standard Code of Jewish law, compiled by Rabbi Yosef Caro in the mid-sixteenth century

Sivan   the third month of the Jewish year

Talmid   (pl. *Talmidim*) disciple, student

Talmud   the sixty volumes of Jewish Law, expounding upon the Torah. It comprises the Mishnah and the (later) discussion and commentary, based on the Mishnah, called the *Gemara*. The terms Talmud and *Gemara* are used interchangeably

Tanya   the classic text of Chabad chasidic thought authored by Rabbi Shneur Zalman of Liadi

Tefillin   small leather boxes, each containing four Torah passages, which the Torah commands adult males to wear daily during the morning prayers

Tehillim   (lit., "praises") the Book of Psalms, authored by King Dovid

Teshuvah   (lit., "return [to God]") repentance

Thirteen Attributes of Mercy   God's boundless capacity for compassion, especially as expressed in the granting of atonement

Torah   the Five Books of Moshe; the *Tanach* (acronym for *Torah, Niveim,* and *Kesuvim,* five books of Moshe, Prophets, and the Writings); or, more broadly, all Jewish writings throughout the ages

Tzaddik   (pl. *tzaddikim*) a righteous or holy person; leader of a chasidic group, a rebbe

Tzedakah   charity

Writings   the third division of the Holy Scriptures, following the Torah (Five Books of Moses) and the Prophets.

YHVH   the special name of God; also called the "four-letter name," the four English letters standing for the Hebrew letters *yud hey vav hey*

Yehoshua   Joshua, the leader of the Jewish people after Moshe

Yeshivah   rabbinical academy

Yetzer Hara   evil inclination

Yetzer Tov   good inclination

Yichudim   unifications; in a technical sense, usually a kabbalistic meditation on one of the letter configurations of the four-letter name of God; the unity of God that's accomplished through the performance of *mitzvos*

Zemirot   devotional *Shabbos* table songs

Zohar   the "Book of Splendor," the central book of the Kabbalah, the Jewish mystical tradition, authored by Rabbi Shimon Bar (ben) Yechai (second century)

Suggested Readings

Buxbaum, Yitzchak. *Jewish Spiritual Practices*. Northvale, NJ: Jason Aronson Inc., 1990.

Kantor, Mattis. *Ten Keys for Understanding Human Nature*. Monsey, NY: Zichron Press, 1994.

Mindel, Nissan. *My Prayer: A Commentary on Daily Prayer*. New York: Kehot, 1972.

Mindel, Nissan. *Philosophy of Chabad*. Vols. 1–2. New York: Kehot, 1973.

Posner, Zalman. *Think Jewish*. Nashville, TN: Kesher Press, 1978.

Schneerson, Joseph I. *Memoirs*. Trans. Nissan Mindel. Vols. 1–2. New York: Kehot, 1956, 1960.

Schneerson, M. M. *Torah Studies*. Adapt. Jonathan Sacks. England: Lubavitch Foundation, 1986.

Schneerson, Menachem M. *Timeless Patterns in Time.*
Trans. Eliyahu Touger. Vol. 1. New York: Kehot,
1993.

Schneerson, Menachem Mendel. *On the Essence of
Chasidus.* Trans. Hershel Greenberg. New York:
Kehot, 1986.

Schneerson, Yosef Yitzchok. *Likkutei Dibburim.*
Trans. Uri Kaploun. Vols. 1–3, New York: Kehot,
1987–1990.

Schochet, J. Immanuel. *The Mystical Dimension.* Vols.
1–3. New York: Kehot, 1990.

Zalman, Shneur. *Likutei Amarim (Tanya).* Bilingual
edition. New York: Kehot, 1973.

Bibliography

Epstein, Yichel Michel. *Aruch Hashulchan*. New York, 1975.

Even Shelemah. Anthology of Teachings of R. Eliyahu of Vilna. Jerusalem, 1960.

Horowitz, Isaiah. *Shaloh, Shnei Luchos Habris*. Jerusalem, 1963.

Ibn Gabbai, Meir. *Avodas Hakodesh*. Jerusalem, 1954.

Karelitz, Abraham Isaiah. *Chazon Ish*. Bnei Brak, 1980.

Medini, Chaim Chizkiyahu. *Sdei Chemed*. Brooklyn, NY, 1959.

Moshe ben Maimon. *Rambam*. Jerusalem, 1959.

Nachmanides, Moshe. *Ramban Al Hatorah*. Jerusalem, 1959.

Schneerson, Menachem Mendel. *Hayom Yom*. Brooklyn, NY, 1961.

Schneerson, Menachem Mendel. *Sefer HaMa'amarim Melukat.* Vols. 1–6. Brooklyn, NY: 1985–1992.

Schneerson, Yosef Yitzchok. *Sefer HaMa'amarim.* Brooklyn, NY, 1945–1990.

Weiner, Moshe. *Hadras Ponim Zokon.* Brooklyn, NY, 1982.

Zalman, Shneur. *Tanya.* Brooklyn, NY, 1965.

Index

239

About the Author

Chaim Yaccov Dalfin received his rabbinical ordination from the Lubavitcher *yeshivah* in Brooklyn, New York. He received his bachelor of religious studies degree from the Rabbinical College of America in Morristown, New Jersey. Rabbi Dalfin is a professor of Jewish Mysticism and Chasidism at the West Coast Talmudic Seminary. He is the author of *Your Better Self* (1994), a book on the chasidic approach to self-improvement, and *Demystifying the Mystical* (1995), a primer to ease the beginner into the esoteric world of mysticism and Chasidism. He is the recording artist of the "Chasidic Melodies Series—Learn, Understand, and Sing." Rabbi Dalfin is a *chasid* of Rabbi Menachem Mendel Schneerson, the Lubavitcher Rebbe. Rabbi Dalfin lectures nationwide on the fundamentals of Chasidus and also leads *farbrengens* with song, stories, and words of inspiration. He was a *mashpia*—spiritual guide—at Yeshiva Ohr Elchanan Chabad in Los Angeles, California. Now he resides with his wife and five children in Brooklyn, New York.